Innovation Mastery

The Definitive Guide to Running the Ultimate Innovation Program

CHRIS KALABOUKIS

Second Edition

Copyright © 2018 Chris Kalaboukis

All rights reserved.

ISBN-13: 978-1727346220
ISBN-10: 172734622X

DEDICATION

For Susan

CONTENTS

Introduction xi

GOOOAL! The Definitive Guide to Developing Outcomes for Your Innovation Program 13

    Goal: Developing New Products 18

    Goal: Filing Patents 20

    Goal: Look Cool to Your Competitors 21

    Goal: Playing with Cool New Toys, But Not Launching Them ... 23

    Goal: Playing Catchup with Your Competitors 24

    Goal: Massive Employee Engagement 26

CULTURE SHOCK: Where does innovation fit in your organization? 29

    Don't Fight It from Without 34

The Players 37

    Executive Sponsor 39

    Program Manager 41

    Technologists 42

    Coders 44

    Marketing 44

    Human Resources 45

    Legal 45

    Inventors 47

Reviewers	49
Approvers	50
A Note on External Programs	50
What's The Upside?	**53**
Experiences	57
Cash	58
Single Inventor	59
Multiple Inventors	59
Access	59
Recognition	60
End Results	**63**
Prototype	64
Product	66
Patent	67
Always Have a Landing Strip	67
What's Patentable?	**69**
Novelty	72
Non-Obviousness	75
Usefulness	76
Visibility	77
Side Effects	**79**

- Change 80
- To Disrupt, Or Not to Disrupt 85
  - Optimal marginality 89
- Inventor Care Program 93
  - Communicate Early, Often and Proactively 95
  - Initial Idea Submission Perfectly Reasonable Responses for Different Scenarios 95
  - Unreasonable Responses 96
  - Tell Them What's Going to Happen, Even If It's Going to Be "Nothing" 96
  - Rewards and Awards 97
  - Do It Very Publicly Within Your Organization 97
  - Serial Inventors 97
- The Tech 99
- The Deets 103
  - Who? 104
  - When? 104
  - Where? 105
  - What? 105
- Up to The Challenge 107
- Exercises 111
  - Exercise I: Hit Up the Science Fiction Bookshelf 113

Exercise II: Make Serendipity Your Good Buddy 114

Exercise III: Get Upset 117

Exercise IV: Take the Maze Backwards 118

Exercise V: Waste Some Time 120

Exercise VI: Go Offline and Make 122

Exercise VII: Have Beginners Mind 124

Exercise VIII: Use the Idea Blender 126

Exercise IX: Face Your Killer 128

Exercise X: Kill the Drag 130

Exercise XI: Be Incongruent 133

Exercise XII: Wander Aimlessly 136

Exercise XIII: Make A Mess 138

Exercise XIV: Change the Nouns 140

Exercise XV: Think Like A Kid 143

Exercise XVI: Repurposing 145

Exercise XVII: Ask "Why Do We Still…" 147

Exercise XVIII: Think Further Out 149

About The Author 151

Let's Talk 153

INTRODUCTION

Thank you.

As a fellow innovation practitioner, I'm happy that you bought this book. It's a culmination of experiences in the trenches running several innovation initiatives for major corporations like Citibank, Google, Hilton, Kellogg's, Walmart, Wells Fargo & Yahoo. I've been a technologist, an innovation specialist for the past 15 years, and a futurist since I was a kid (before I even knew what the word meant). I love seeing what's next and developing new products and services for that future.

Along the way, I've come across both guides and obstacles, and I firmly believe that anyone, anywhere, no matter the size or age or vertical of the organization, can invent new products and services which can radically change their companies.

People crave action on their ideas. The worst thing you can be is indifferent to your people's ideas. Your employees are happiest when they make a difference.

Even a small dent in the universe makes a huge difference.

CHAPTER 1

GOOOAL! THE DEFINITIVE GUIDE TO DEVELOPING OUTCOMES FOR YOUR INNOVATION PROGRAM

The room was hushed.

The presenter had just completed a very thorough presentation of using their tool to develop a robust innovation program, and with all the fixings. The goals were clearly set out, the right people were involved at every level of the organization (they had not one but two executive sponsors), the plan to reward the inventors was fully fleshed out and funded, the processes used to capture and review the ideas was set, a plan to funnel those ideas into the product or patent pipeline was nailed, and the marketing plan to communicate everything was detailed out. The program was launched, ran well with only a few minor glitches, and both the prototype and patent pipelines were full of interesting ideas. Employees had enjoyed the program, competing and collaborating with each other to brainstorm some fantastic ideas, which were now sitting, ready to be built in the product pipeline, and invention disclosure forms were being filled out for some of the more far forward-thinking ideas, so that they could capture the IP even if they weren't able to build the products immediately. News of the program had leaked into the press, and even analysts were looking at the company in a new light – could they innovate their ways out of their doldrums?

The snappily dressed presenter finished her presentation and asked, "Any questions?"

There was a pause.

Suddenly, a man who had been sitting in the second row stood up. He looked a bit like a reporter of old: jeans, white shirt, corduroy jacket, maybe a little disheveled. He gave his name and his company name, a large, well respected consumer goods company.

"Great presentation, thanks. But…" he said.

"Where is the value?"

I think I may have heard a collective groan from the crowd. The presenter looked nervous. The questioner looked pointedly at the presenter.

And the presenter started on what I call the good old "value of innovation song and dance."

- "Hard to quantify."
- "Intangible benefits."
- "Employee morale."
- "Number of products."
- "Number of patents."
- "Analyst feelings."

And the questioner kept hammering.

"Waste of money." – "Waste of resources" – "What's the bottom line?" – "Where are the revenues?" – "Where are the savings?"

All, of course, leading to the unasked question:

"Why should we innovate, if there is no direct link to the bottom line?"

Soon, the presenter's time ran out, and I'm sure she was thankful to leave the stage. I found her afterwards and told her that she did a pretty good job considering. We had a good discussion over the question – and it seems that yes: for some people, it is a tough question to answer:

"Why innovate?"

So, I thought: I love tough questions. Let me take a crack at this one.

Where Do You Want to Go Today?

I love this tagline. I think it was the tagline that Microsoft used back in 1995 when they first launched Windows 95 or some other version of Windows. It's a simple question: tell me your destination, inferring that with Microsoft Windows, you can get there.

Tell me your destination.

How often do we hit the road without really knowing where we are going to go? Do you get dressed, put your shoes on, leave your house, lock your door, get in your car and drive? Not very often, right? If we pretty much know where we need to go before we get in the car, why don't we do the same before we launch innovation programs?

Why do we innovate? There are so many intangible benefits which come out of an innovation program, for some of us who understand how the intangible benefits far outweigh the tangible benefits, we groan when we hear someone talk about the value or the connection to the bottom line. How can you put a value on innovation? It's, like the old MasterCard ad, priceless.

Nevertheless, not everyone gets that. My hunch is that most of the decision makers within your organization are a bit stricter when it comes to results: if they spend $X on an innovation program unless it delivers a product which returns 10X or 100X, they aren't interested. They want billion-dollar businesses, right out of the gate.

Of course, its exceptionally difficult to capture all the benefits of an innovation program and translate them directly back to dollars: how do you capture the fact that your employees might spend a bit longer thinking about new ways to optimize your product to save you money, or when they feel proud (and work harder) working for an innovative company? Or when they can tell you about minor improvements and new features which could improve the customer experience, leading to more referrals and new business.

Many, if not most, of these paths, are untraceable – innovation in general amps up everyone's game – in so many ways, that you may never be able to say that $X spent brought us back 10X in revenues or 5X in stock price. You may not be able to trace everything.

But there are some things that you can trace. You get to these by starting with that question Microsoft asked 20 years ago: "Where do you want to go today?"

GOOOOOOAL!

Set goals, or outcomes if you will, which ARE traceable.

First, determine a few measures of success. Some are easy, and are trackable with your even most simplistic innovation management system:

- Number of ideas generated
- Number of employees involved
- Number of comments received
- Number of ideas per employee (ideal in identifying your serial inventors)
- Number of patents filed (if you are looking to do this, of course)
- Number of ideas to prototype

I'm sure that there are many other solid metrics you could capture. You can always try to look for the diamond in the rough, that single new idea, which when built and launched, pays for everything preceding it, rare but doable.

What will most likely happen: your company will be improved in many more immeasurable ways. These are difficult, but not impossible to track.

What are your big goals for the program? These tie back to what innovation means to you. What does innovation mean to you?

- Develop real new products, some of which may make tons of money?

- File patents for products you might build or license? (which may eventually make ton loads of money)

- Look cool among your competitors? (which may make your stock look more attractive and maybe improve the chances of you hiring great talent?)

- Playing with cool new toys, but not launching them? (not sure what this will do other than waste time, (which is not always a bad thing – see exercises in Chapter 14) unless all your employees get to play with the toys too, leading to even more innovation and helping you to hire more cool people)

- Playing catchup to your competitors? (which you should position as leapfrogging your competitors – if poor African countries can leapfrog the first world with cool new mobile apps and services, then you should be able to out-innovate your competitors to leapfrog in front of them. It happens more than you think.)

- Massive employee engagement? (make your employees super happy by listening and doing something about the ideas they've come up with)

Or maybe it's all the above? Let's look at each of these in detail:

Goal: Developing New Products

If your goal is to develop new products, the metrics are easy on this one, simply track the number of ideas which make it through the pipeline from idea to product. If this is your goal, then you need to invest the time, money and resources to make sure that these ideas get through the pipeline to product or at least a prototype that you can throw into the marketplace (even a small, limited marketplace) and see what happens. Don't spend your entire budget on the program itself, save some of it for the product development, marketing and management of the trial.

It's important to be very cognizant of the operational voices, who will try to come in at this point and shut down prototypes, products, and trials which will have no immediate perceived value proposition. If the founders of Twitter or Snapchat had done that, there would be no Twitter ($17B valuation) or Snapchat ($16B valuation). Make sure that you can spend the money to get it out the door, and let it ride for a while.

The founders of WhatsApp were thinking of shutting it down a few months before it went viral. Remember that it was bought by Facebook for $22B shortly after? Would you let your operational voices (some people call these the corporate innovation immune system) shut down what could be a $22B product, all for the sake of a lack of budget? We are shooting for the moon – we should be allowed to spend a few bucks to get there.

In my experience, many enterprises let their operational voices shut down their innovative voices, expecting something for nothing. Unless the product is an immediate viral success with tons of traction and revenue, we should shut it down right away. I've seen too many awesome products go that way, only to be launched by a startup a few months later to huge traction and potential revenues. Don't be that innovation program: be ready for the operational voices to throw up a very strong case to shut you down early, sounding the hue and cry that "this won't make any money." Don't let them stop you before you've even started.

Goal: Filing Patents

This one is a little easier and a little harder. Easier because you don't need to think about building the product and a little harder because you need to make sure that you are developing something that a) is patentable and b) you will be able to extract value out of sometime at least four years from now. There is a cost involved as well, and your legal team will also need to be able to have the capabilities to manage outside counsel who will probably do most of the filing for you.

You can easily track this one as well: how many patents did you file? Some companies get into competition with their competitors on this one. Of course, it is important to have quality patents as well, but with patents, you typically never really know which idea will be valuable when you are filing it – so the number of patents is a good metric.

This is a tough one for companies who don't think long term. It will take about 4-5 years for your patent to be issued, and once its issued, you can then license it or sell it. The cost to file a patent is typically in a $15k range, unless your company files many patents already and they are able to get something like a "volume discount", paying $15k per idea for something that "might" show some value 5 years from now (5 years is like a bazillion in tech years, no?) is sometimes even a harder pill to swallow for some companies than the product goal above.

Then there are the patentability criteria: novelty, usefulness, and non-obviousness, there is one more which we like to look for as well, which is visibility. There is more detail later in the book, but in short the idea has to be new (no one else has really thought of this specific idea), useful (it has to be something which people will generally think is useful – this is why you can't really patent a painting, even though they may be useful in calming your soul) and non-obvious (if your invention is something which is just an obvious extension of something someone else thought of – like using handlebars in your car instead of a steering wheel). Visible – the idea is something that can be seen out there – for example, you may be able to patent an algorithm for a better search engine, but if you can't figure out if someone is infringing on your idea because you can't tell, then the value of the patent is typically not very high.

However, if you are enough of a long-term thinker to wait it out – this is a good strategy. Make sure that you also have a reward program for your inventors at filing, AND at issuance, so that they get rewarded at both ends – might even be an incentive for them to stay with you.

Goal: Look Cool to Your Competitors

An interesting goal. But it shouldn't be your primary goal.

Unfortunately, I've personally experienced something that feels like this: you have put together a very well thought out program, with seemingly the right people, processes and tools in place. You market the program, you run the program, get great ideas out of the program, but then the ideas seem to languish in the system without going anywhere. At the same time, you have many of the executives in the organization talking about how innovative they are, talk about the initiatives, like this one, talk about the great numbers of ideas generated and the number of employees engaged.

But that's as far as it goes. There isn't even any real talk of any of the products generated, you seem to hear the word innovation, innovative and innovator repeatedly in the marketing materials, but nothing to back it up.

Where are the innovative products and services? What is this cool stuff that you are developing?

Of course, since the point of the program is to look cool, it seems like you are just trying to out innovate each other by blasting the word "innovation" from every loudspeaker than you can.

Talking the talk, but not walking the walk.

I'm all for touting every innovative product that you've developed from the rooftops. But first, let it be REAL. If you are worried about the IP – protect it via patent filing first.

Stop saying that you are being innovative, BE INNOVATIVE. You don't hear Google saying that they are innovative. You hear Apple saying it, though.

Innovate so that you can look cool in comparison to your competitors: it has many, many intangible benefits (and maybe a few you can measure)

- People will see your company in a new light

- It may become easier to hire more innovative individuals, thus generating more innovative products and services

- Many innovators prefer "doing cool stuff" instead of "big salaries" so you might even see some relief there

- If you are a public company, analysts might see you in a new light. If you are a large public company who may be seen as a has-been, overtaken by newer, cooler companies with more interesting products, maybe building some cool, new products and getting them out the door might go a long way towards revising their opinion of you. Innovation can even save you.

- You will get more favorable press – everyone loves innovation. As an example, check out the video that Amazon put out about drone delivery. They teased us with that in 2013, but nothing came of it. Now we are seeing full on video demonstrations of a real drone supposedly delivering a new pair of shoes. You can measure by reviewing your press mentions and "innovation."

Goal: Playing with Cool New Toys, But Not Launching Them

It's Christmas morning. You are six. You could barely sleep thinking about all the presents which might be under the tree. Is it that new BB gun you always wanted? Will Santa be good to you this year? Does your dad have a present under the tree which looks like a crate labelled "fragilé"? Your mind races with the thought of all the cool new toys that might be under the tree. You're under the covers, wide awake, waiting with anxious anticipation for the moment your Mom calls upstairs "Wow! Look at all the presents Santa brought!". You fling off the covers and tear downstairs, only to be greeting with the most amazing site of your young life, the Christmas tree surrounded by what seems likes hundreds of presents!

You hope none of them are clothes.

Who doesn't love playing with cool new toys?

Playing with cool new toys, if you ask me, is one of the best parts of running an innovation program. It's an awesome side effect of working on the latest and greatest stuff. One of the main reasons I moved to Silicon Valley from the Great White North was not just to get away from the snow and ice in the winter and the blazing heat and humidity in the summer, but it was to work with, play with and help invent all the coolest new toys.

Playing with cool new toys/products/services is awesome. Inventing them is even cooler! But is it the main goal of your innovation program? A great side benefit, and definitely a major draw for those innovators who love to work with the cool, new toys (as I mentioned above, I know plenty of people are more in the business to build new things, to make a dent in the universe, as opposed to getting a big chunk of cash in the IPO)– that helps too of course.

Inventing the future is cool – inventing so that you can be the first to play with them, but not turn them into anything real, not so cool.

Think of it this way: you are a typical employee in a typical enterprise. You have an awesome idea for a new product, you submit it into the program, it gets accepted and built, and is being used internally to show off how cool your company is. How do you think you would feel?

In my experience, inventors would forgo almost any kind of reward in return for one thing: to be able to point to their product, in the real world, a living breathing thing which people are using, and say to themselves, their families, their children, their friends, three little words:

"I made that"

Help them to say that. Launch those cool new things into the world.

Goal: Playing Catchup with Your Competitors

Alas, people and corporations can be similar in some ways. Just like you can come across people with low self-esteem, there are corporations with low self-esteem out there as well. Some companies feel that they are so far behind on the innovation front, that was is no way that they could catch up with their competitors. They look at where their competitors are about them: they may have much cooler, more modern products with a more up-to-date look-and-feel. Their competitors may have way more patent applications in the queue, as well as issued patents which they filed years ago, so it would be tough for them to file anything new in that space. Or they might look at their user base and realize that they are losing traction to competitors who maybe have much more uptake by up and coming demographics, like Millennials or Gen Z.

They feel that they are so far behind that there is no way that they can catch up. They feel that if they can at least have a product set which can match their competitors, then at least they may have a fighting chance to at least get some market share back. But if you ask me, they've thrown in the towel before they have even stepped into the ring. Are you familiar by any chance with M-Pesa?

When I say Africa – what comes to mind? Starving children? Ethnic, religious and tribal strife? Terrible living conditions – rampant disease? Or do you think – "some of the most innovative products in the world?" It's the latter.

Several years ago, most of Africa was the former. Poor telecommunications, poor infrastructure, a poor populace, ethnic and religious wars. Sure, there are still some areas like that. But, in many ways, they've leapfrogged us in the first world by being able to apply new technologies without the baggage that we have.

They took a green field and planted it with new mobile products and services. If you visited Nairobi, you might see a metropolis even more advanced than San Francisco or New York, with the inhabitants sporting cutting edge mobile phone technologies and products and services so forward thinking they've never fly in heavily regulated environments like the United States.

The Kenyans get it: they can innovate not just because they need to, they can innovate more effectively since they have less constraints on what they can and cannot do. Constraints which we impose upon ourselves when we say "we can't" or "don't go there."

Did you know that the whole cable TV business was born in theft? When I first went to work for a Canadian cable TV company (which was eventually bought by Shaw Communications) they ran a little educational session about the beginnings of the cable TV industry. Apparently, way back when TV signals were transmitted over the air, you needed a pretty good antenna to capture the signal. Really good antennas where not that cheap, so people were stuck watching things with poor reception.

Some enterprising individuals bought antennas and were getting pretty good signal. So, they thought, "Hmm I'm getting a good signal. What if I ran a cable with the signal in it to my neighbor's house? I wonder if they would pay for a share of my signal?" Well he did, and his other neighbors did, and soon the cable business was born: they grabbed signal out of the air via big badass antennae, then sold it to their neighbors.

Thing is, it wasn't exactly legal: the operators were taking someone else's broadcast and selling it – with nothing going back to the broadcaster. They were stealing the signal and reselling it, but it wasn't formally enforced back then. By the time the government wanted to enforce it, the cable companies had grown so big and made so much money that they could easily start to pay the broadcasters fees for distributing their content.

My point? Don't simply think that innovation can get you to parity with your competitors – innovation can help you to leapfrog over your competitors into completely new markets where you can leave them in the dust.

Think out of the box you put yourself and your competitors in. With innovation, build your box where you will prevail.

The 22 Immutable Laws of Marketing still prevail today. If you can't compete in their box, make your own. And when you do, don't be afraid to push your boundaries.

Goal: Massive Employee Engagement

Why don't we look at the life of Jane Employee? Jane wakes up at 4:30 am every morning. Jane makes a cup of coffee at 4:45 am. She leaves for boot camp at 5:15 am. She does a Cross-Fit style boot camp from 5:30 am to 6:15 am. She goes home, showers, gets dressed, drives to the train station gets on the train and starts reading a trashy novel on her Kindle for the hour-long commute. She gets off the train, then takes the streetcar to the office. She gets to the office, pours herself another cup of coffee, and sits at her desk for 8-10 hours. She is so busy that she can barely ever step away for lunch, and her job may be tedious to a fault.

However, she, like all your employees, has a super quick mind, and continuously comes up with better ways to do things, better features and functions for your current products, and even new products that you could sell. But she works in accounting, and when she attempted to approach her boss to tell her about some of her ideas, she was told to drop them because they were just in accounting and no one on the product side of the business cared about what people in accounting thought.

Replicate that with every other department other than the product side, and you have a lot of unhappy, unmotivated employees, all with great ideas. Same goes for if you have one of those "innovation labs," those rare places with special people who only spend time coming up with new ideas – no one else innovates, or typically the C-suite "thinks" that no one else can innovate, when everyone innovates, all the time.

Running an enterprise wide crowdsourced innovation program is a great way to motivate your employees – in addition to developing great new products and services, if the program is properly designed, developed and run, with all the communications channels running smoothly, it can be one of the most effective motivational programs your company has ever run.

When else can you ask your employees to help you design and define the future of your company? When else can your CEO connect directly with your entire organization and get feedback and ideas from every corner of the company? In what other way can you entice your employees to participate in a positive way and, with the proper communication in place, involve your employees deeply and compellingly?

No other way that I can imagine. It's positive, and even a message that may help present your upper management as more human and vulnerable, reaching out to say, "We need your help." What better way is there to tie your employee's future into your corporate future by letting them participate in the future product development process.

Engaging your employees is a fantastic secondary effect of designing and developing a robust, effective crowdsourced innovation program.

There you have it:

The right goals:

- Developing real new products and services, or features to make your current products more compelling
- Filing patents for products you might build or license
- Employee engagement

The wrong goals:

- Looking cool among your competitors
- Playing with cool new toys, but not launching them
- Playing catch up to your competitors (when you can leapfrog them instead)

Now that you know which goals to set, you are ready to begin.

CHAPTER 2

CULTURE SHOCK: WHERE DOES INNOVATION FIT IN YOUR ORGANIZATION?

"They shut it down."

He whispered the phrase to me reverently, with a touch of sadness. My colleague just met with me over lunch to tell me that they had decided to shutter the innovation lab. It had only been around for two years and had done some awesomely interesting stuff, but for some reason, its time was up.

"Why?" I asked. Of course, I knew the answer but was curious about what was the straw that broke the camel's back. I'd heard about the issues that the lab had since its founding.

I thought back to the announcement of the lab by the new CEO. It was the beginning of a new, more innovative company, he said. We will build an innovation lab and stock it with the best and brightest. We will even put it somewhere else physically, far away from us here in the normal campus. We will give them the leeway to innovate, to come up with new, disruptive ideas and innovations. I could still remember him on the stage at the all hands meeting – he'd brought the new director of the new lab onstage with him, and they were sharing the limelight. He introduced the new director, and the director went right into it. He went into a very passionate speech, speckled profusely with phrases like:

- Disruption!   Innovation!   Disruptive Innovation!
- Out-of-the-box Thinking! Break out of our current mindset!
- Everything is on the table! No holds barred!

At the end, he smiled, and everyone applauded. Yes, we thought, we'll be cool again! This lab will create some awesome new products and show the world that we can kick ass too! Hey, thought about half of the crowd, I wonder if I can get a job in the lab! The other half resented the lab, wondering why we couldn't just innovate on our own. But at least, together, right now, we thought, don't we work for a cool company?

That was two years ago. Since then, the innovation lab HAD been on a winning streak. They quickly settled in and hired both outside innovators and transferred people from other groups. They moved in to a new, super cool office space in SOMA San Francisco. The place was huge, open plan, lots of exposed brick. Just being in the space makes you feel more creative. Just escaping from the cube farm of the rest of the company made you feel great. There were whiteboards everywhere, desks and table strewn around in random space, no straight lines everywhere – everything strategically placed for maximum collaboration and creativity generation.

Did you know that they did a study where they asked two sets of college students to solve a problem? They gave both sets of students the same problem, but before they were told to sit down and solve it, they ask one group to walk up and down the room in straight lines, and they asked the other group to walk randomly around the room and in curves. Once they'd done that for a bit, they asked them to sit down and figure out the problem. Guess which groups came up with the more creative solutions?

The Lab was an awesome, innovation space. Once opened, they quickly decided that they wanted to move faster than the rest of the company, so they decided to develop things in the most modern, rapid application development languages and frameworks available. They would do super agile work in rapid iterations with everyone in the room, lean startup style. They came up with and generated tons of prototypes, using the rapid pace of agile development, coupled with the ease of using the new frameworks, they were able to develop a whole new raft of software prototypes in no time. Of course, they weren't scalable, but they were able to place them in front of both internal and external focus groups to a great response.

The press loved it as well – here is a venerable company finally looking like it was going to generate some cool, new, innovative new products. Not only was the Lab a hit with the press, they, and other innovation pundits were actively promoting this vision that the company that they had created as the new model for innovation.

"This is what innovative companies need," they all said, "Don't wait to be disrupted by your competitors, build your internal lab and disrupt yourself."

They trucked on like this for what seemed like a long time, receiving accolade after accolade, mostly from external sources. But there was trouble brewing.

I wasn't in the group, but I kept an eye on them since I've always been interested in innovation and building new product and services, thinking that they might be the group to get our company out of the funk it's been in.

This group wasn't quiet about their successes; it talked openly about the cool new products it was building right out on their blog (but only after provisional patent applications were filed on them). One of the first applications to come out of the group was a location finding service, something that would likely become a keystone platform service in the world that was becoming increasingly more mobile. They put a small prototype on the web, and everyone loved it. The president of our company praised the product as well, both internally and in the press, and talked about how it would be the first of many new products to come out of the new Lab.

The product was a hit all around, but as I mentioned, they didn't have the coders to make it a real scalable product, it was a very cool, proof-of-concept prototype, which, as far as everyone concerned, proved the concept. The go ahead was given to launch the product, once it was made scalable.

The product was handed back to the company proper to build into a scalable, launchable version. They took one look at the code and said "This is crap. We can't use this. Not only is this not written in our preferred language and framework, we don't have the time or budget to rewrite it from scratch. We will have to try and fit it in with all of the other work we are doing." A few months later, all the chatter around the product was gone, and it was never heard from again.

Just the first battle. The valiant director of the Lab kept going – they kept developing prototypes of the coolest, most interesting stuff. Some of it moved forward, others didn't, but as time went by, it seemed inevitable that no matter what the group generated, no matter how cool or interesting or innovative the product was, no matter how much innovation cred the company got from the outside, nothing that the groups built was ever going to launch.

That was the last few years. The day was finally here when they had decided that the grand experiment was over.

What happened? Simple. The corporate immune system killed it. It detected a disturbance in the Force and sent its midichlorians to destroy it, or something like that. When they finally shuttered the Lab, the new president (yes, we'd lost the guy who launched the Lab, but it wasn't his fault it failed) announced that it was a great experiment, and they learned a lot from it. We didn't need to "lock up" innovation in a small, forward thinking group, "innovation was everywhere, and that it was all of our jobs to be innovative." I think the stock price dropped that day too.

Ah, corporate culture. On bad days, sometimes you think, as Sartre did at the end of "No Exit" that "hell is other people" on other days you think, hmm, they are not so bad.

Is your culture ready to innovate?

I do feel that innovation is everyone's responsibility. Just like growth shouldn't just remain in the hands of the sales and marketing folks, everyone can and should innovate. But the question really should be – are you interested in innovation? Is innovation in your DNA?

Typically, companies who began via an innovative idea, begin with a highly innovative culture. All bets are off, out-of-the-box thinking is what built the firm, and it's what kept it strong at the beginning. Its one of the reasons why startups have very few issues innovating – well, I guess it depends on the startup. There are plenty of businesses that don't need to be innovative, they do perfectly well and are profitable serving their current niche.

Think of the hundreds of thousands of businesses in the small to medium size enterprise space. Many of them have defined their marketspace, be it by demographic, location or other factors, and do quite well in that space, without really innovating because they don't have to. You don't need to innovate to be successful. You need to have a product market fit – which is a fancy way of saying you are creating or providing something that someone wants to buy.

Whether you are or not, either way, you need to keep moving forward and innovating, but how do you do it in a culture like the one I've described above – how do you innovate when the corporate immune system is constantly trying to shut you down? You must take culture into account.

Don't Fight It from Without

In the example above, that company made a huge show of creating a new Lab which gave the company some cache and made it look interesting, at least for a while to the outside world. However, it also showed a perfect example of not taking in internal corporate culture into account. While the new head of the innovation lab was well meaning, what did he think the rest of the company was going to feel like when he came in, all guns blazing, trying to pull the company culture forward forcibly? Of course, he would feel like an invading force, trying to change what seemed to be working well (or at least well enough) for a long time.

People had spent a lot of time and effort putting together communications structure to keep the hierarchy in place, to keep those lines of communications as is. It came in like a threat to the system, so it is no surprise that it ended that way.

Let me give you another example. We came in to a company to restart a moribund innovation program which had launched a few months earlier and had some great initial traction but now was just sort of stalling. There were many problems with the program, some of which had to do with the software that they have selected in order to run the program – and the company that they selected to assist them with the program simply installed the software and basically left the guy in charge to take it the rest of the way – and he based the program on the way the software operated. The problem here was twofold – one, the software was not a fit for the organization (it was focused on a phased approach, with very little transparency between those who submitted the idea and those who voted and commented on the idea). I'm sure that the software and the process the software used might have been great for a manufacturing company or maybe a medical device company, but for a freewheeling, more fun and open company, it was wrong. That was one of the problems.

The other was the way the program itself was structured. There was little feedback and communication, and the prizes awarded were, in some quarters, considered unworthy. Why give out free iPads when most of your people already have them?

Culture will kill any program if you don't get it right. Spend some time at the very beginning of the process determining what will work within the system. Run some focus groups within the company to determine what is going wrong and what people need. Hit those pain points when to kick off or revise the program. Even better yet, do a cultural scan to ensure that you are ready to innovate.

We ended up rewriting the software to the company's specifications – it went from a dull looking web-based version of Windows software to a cool, reddit style web app, allowing anyone, anywhere to submit, vote and comment on ideas. We revised the prizes to be more experiential – we gave the top inventors the opportunity to lunch with the president and gave the rest of the inventors what they considered the best award of all: RECOGNITION.

That's what it was like for this specific company. It may be different for yours — I can help you with what will or will not work. You need to work within your corporate culture and see where it can bend and don't push too hard. Otherwise, it will break.

Be prepared for things to not move as quickly as you'd like or get the results you want right away. It takes time.

One day though, you will see the results of your efforts — maybe it's that call from a remote office thanking you profusely for allowing them to have a voice at HQ, or the CEO stopping by your table at lunch to give you a pat on the back, or maybe one of the ideas generated was sent to the team for implementation.

Finally, make sure that if you have a lab which builds prototypes, try and maintain the same or similar framework to what is currently the standard at your company. I've seen many situations when the labs use the latest and great agile tech to create phenomenal products, which everyone gives the go ahead to build and scale, but then they die for lack of support after the fact. Make sure that you have a place for these ideas to go — even if you must split off some of the team from the lab to go and shepherd them to reality

CHAPTER 3

THE PLAYERS

"People are people

So why should it be

You and I should get along so awfully."

   - Depeche Mode

I love Depeche Mode. As a guy who grew up in the 80s, there was nothing better that kicking back and listening to my old record player, reading Jean-Paul Sartre and Albert Camus and think, aren't people horrible?

As you may be able to tell, I used to be a very serious introvert. Now I think I've changed a bit, but I still get this nagging feeling that everything that ever goes wrong with almost anything is someone's fault.

At one company I was at, the most popular idea submitted was "fire half of the middle management." You think this guy may have had a bone to pick with some people?

This section is about the people who are essential to the success of your innovation program or lab, the key essential personnel you need to make it a success:

1. Executive Sponsor, or preferably sponsors
2. Program Manager
3. Technologists
4. Coders
5. Marketing
6. Human Resources
7. Legal

8. Inventors
9. Reviewers
10. Approvers

In this chapter, we'll dive deep into the roles that we believe you need to have a successful program, as well as some other people issues. Some of the roles above you'll find in multiple individuals, in others they may be teams of people. If you ask us, the more people that you can pull in to support your program, the better.

Executive Sponsor

You need an executive sponsor. Let me say that again: you need an executive sponsor. It is nonnegotiable. You need more than one executive sponsor. Based on our experience, the number one killer of innovation labs and innovation programs is losing their executive sponsor. We have seen this far too many times.

It doesn't matter if your program is doing well or flailing – without an executive sponsor, your days are short.

If you are looking to start a program, before you do anything, get an executive sponsor. You don't have to build up a huge case for it since it's almost impossible to show an ROI on possible future innovation unless you are already showing an ROI on current innovation efforts. Put together a short deck describing the program that you want to set up and pitch it to your most receptive boss who can run it up the chain. Be persistent, and eventually, you should find an executive sponsor. If you can't find one in the C-Suite, you still may have a chance to start a smaller program, but your chances of success are lower. If you can't find a sponsor no matter how hard you try, then we have some bad news for you. Your company may not be ready or able to run an innovation program. If you are still interested in running an innovation program, you may need to scale it down to your group. You may even have to leave your company.

There is nothing more frustrating than attempting to drag a company into a more innovative culture if your senior leaders are not ready for it.

If your program is already running and you have a sponsor, that's great. Take my advice: get more. These days, in fact in any days, in my experience the moment there is any uncertainty about the markets, the company or its future, then the first thing to go is the innovation program. Innovation is considered a "nice to have" and only seems to flourish in good times, and is almost always cut in lean times, (or even if lean times are on the horizon) so if you really want your program or lab to live on, no matter what happens, you will need to spread the sponsorship duties across a number of people. Additionally, with all the M&A activity and executive shuffling that tends to go on in some larger organizations, it is always a good idea to have more than one sponsor.

If you had a sponsor and have recently lost them, maybe they've been reassigned, or maybe let go, or maybe they've left the company and you currently have no sponsor, you should be prepared for the program to either be shuttered or try your hardest to get a new sponsor as soon as possible. An innovation program without an executive sponsor likely has a short shelf life.

Why is this? When everyone keeps saying that innovation is so important to an organization, you might think, so do I need a sponsor?

The issue is that, no matter how well you attempt to integrate your innovation function into the culture of your organization, there will always be factions within your company who are ready to kick you out of the organization or shut you down. The organizations which find innovation nonthreatening are few are far between. You can always tell those organizations because even their organizational structures can be innovative. If you are seeing a standard ordinary org chart in your organization, then there is a good chance that someone out there still wants to shut you down.

Program Manager

Once you have secured your sponsor, you will need a program manager to create and run the program. I'm assuming that's you.

Good Luck!

OK, I'm kidding. (I'm not.) The fact is that while you may have the toughest role, keeping all this moving forward, you also have the most rewarding. There is nothing like seeing the ideas submitted by your inventors being viewed and reviewed. There is nothing like the amazing engagement and excitement a program like this elicits among your employees. There is nothing like the thrill when you hear how someone's idea was selected from so many others to become a real product or go into the patent pipeline. When you see your inventors, your employees, joining in, excited and engaged with the future directions of your company. No longer are they simply pushing bits around but are truly contributing to the future welfare of your company. It's a great feeling.

Of course, on the flip side, there are many barriers to overcome, but your role is to manage everything that comes along, knock down those barriers, and keep moving forward. You will:

1. Design the parameters of the program and identify the executive sponsor

2. Work with your internal marketing team to define a theme for the program which fits your culture. The positioning of the program is extremely important to its success. Some people feel that it's all about the tool and the processes used to capture and process the ideas but, its more about the overall program than it is about the technology.

3. Work with your HR people to position this as an employee engagement program as well as an ideation program, as well

an educational and training program. As I mentioned in Chapter 1, an innovation program, especially an enterprise wide program, has an amazing ability to engage even the most jaded workforce, if it's done properly (otherwise known as "following the principles in this book")

4. Work with your legal team to determine your patent outcomes. Depending on your company's current stance on intellectual property (which we will cover more in chapter 6) you may be completely prepared to funnel patentable ideas

As the program manager, you are the key to making this whole thing work. No pressure! But seriously, there may be some days when you are ready to give up, some days when you feel like you are battling the entire company to move a few steps forward, some days when you truly wonder if people mean what they say when they say, "innovate or die." Sometimes it will feel like the inverse, that your organization desperately needs to innovate.

We've all read the *Innovator's Dilemma* and understand that competitive forces will eventually overcome a company that does not innovate and die. We all understand (well, most of us do anyways) that innovation is not a force to be feared, but the next evolutionary step in your company's future. Your innovation program is the womb which will birth new products, new services and eventually new companies to replace your own. If you can think of it that way, innovation and disruption is a natural way of life. We disrupted our parents and our children will disrupt us, and so on.

OK, let's move on to the rest of your team:

Technologists

When you do get a program up and running, you will need a tool to capture, sort and review those ideas. While there are many tools like that on the market (from simple to the complex), you will likely need someone from IT to assist you in the selection of an innovation management system.

There are many tools on the market, and you will need to select a tool which will map to your corporate culture. Therefore, it is important to nail the outcomes and the culture fit first: if you use a tool which does not map to the culture, it will introduce drag, and you don't need any more drag than is necessary.

As I mentioned earlier, we were brought in to reboot a moribund program at one of our clients, and the tool that they used was a big stumbling block. All the other tools that the client used were cool and cutting edge; this one looked like it was Windows 3.1 app which had been turned into a webpage. Beyond the look and feel (even though the design and workflow of the tool is extremely important – there have been so many programs which fall flat due to poor interface design) the process and transparency options were sorely lacking. Here we were trying to foist a backwards looking, closed process system tool on a leading-edge user base. When it launched, it collected a few ideas, but nowhere near what it could have had it been the right tool for the job. Think of it this way: this is how your inventors will interact with your innovation program. The interface must be as cool and slick as the rest of your program, and a fit to the culture of your organization.

You need a technologist to assist you in selecting a tool. You may already have a tool in-house which does this kind of thing (at one client we ran a tool review without realizing that they already had seven licenses of a perfectly good tool which they were using in a completely different area of the organization). If you don't have a tool, the technologist can assist you in selecting and configuring the tool to your specifications and process. Don't be timid here: the success of your program depends on the tool being able to accurately communicate the theme and process involved in the program, ask for what you need to be successful.

Depending on your industry, you may have many different levels of review and approval in the ideation and review process. However, our most successful implementations have been ones where the most transparency and the most communications occurred.

In later chapters, we'll talk about the pluses and minuses of specific tools, but at this point, make sure that you attempt to work with a technologist who understands that the program itself is more important that the tool itself. Most importantly, the functionality of the tool should not dictate the process of the program.

Coders

While this is rare in our experience, you may be in a truly forward-thinking company which understands that if there are some interesting ideas which come out of your innovation program, then some of those ideas will need to move to the prototype stage to garner enough support to develop into a real live product. If you have the luxury of being able to create a team who can also develop prototypes of the ideas submitted and approved, then you will need coders to do the work. These coders can be part of your team, or if you have Google style 20% time, then they can come from other teams, and it can be their 20% time. In the best case, the inventors who've come up with the idea can also help you code the idea. Ideally, here you need at least one front end developer who can design beautiful interfaces (the interface design is more key than covering all the functionality) and a backend developer who can make it work. Don't worry about scalability, use a rapid prototyping framework to generate a beautiful working prototype. You can then use this prototype to pitch the idea for product.

Marketing

We've never been able to create, launch and run a successful program without some marketing assistance. You need marketing to sell your program, keep it top of mind for the duration of the program, help you to come up with the theme and materials of the program, and generally assist in building communications and outreach. You can use marketing personnel who typically talk to your customers, or ideally internal communications folks who already have the pulse of your internal corporate culture. You may be able to do it on your own if you have a marketing background, but we suggest that you get help here – you want the program to look professional, and there is nothing like professional designer's touch. You will need a theme, imagery which matches that theme, copy which matches that theme, and a communications plan which describes what you say when and to whom.

Human Resources

An enterprise wide crowdsourced innovation program is a phenomenal motivating force for employees. If your HR department is receptive (and we have come across some who aren't), they will be one of your biggest allies in assisting, you in spreading the word about your program. They can help you with selecting awards for participation, communicating with employees, making sure that you don't step on any landmines with awards (there are some companies who have very specific rules when it comes to what you can and cannot reward your employees with – iPads maybe, recognition for sure, wild drunken trips to Vegas, probably not.)

The HR department can also be a foe; test the waters with them early and make sure that you keep them as allies.

Ally with everyone. You already have enough hidden (and some not so hidden) forces trying to take your program down, why make any more enemies?

Legal

You need to consult with legal on two fronts.

One, you must ensure that whoever will join into the program has properly agreed to release their rights to any intellectual property that they generate for the program. Most employees have already done this, (its typically handled during the onboarding process) but in some cases, if might be unclear when it comes to contractors. While typically all contractors also sign terms when they come on that all of their work is work for hire and that the work product, including any ideas that they come up with when they are engaged with the company automatically become the company's property, in some cases, your legal department may wish to restrict participation in the program to only full-time employees additionally. Even though some of your contractors may have great ideas, there is likely too much a of legal risk to allow them into the program. Every time we have come across this issue, contractors have not been allowed to participate.

Two, if you are lucky, some of the ideas which your people will generate will be so amazingly cool that they will be patentable. If that is the case, your legal team will determine the patentability of the idea (although there is some detail on what is and isn't patentable later in this book) and if it is patentable, they may file a patent for the idea.

We suggest that even if you are not looking for patentable ideas, you will get some – ideas that are so cool and far out and probably not buildable today but at some future time and with some future system. These ideas may be something that your company may do in future, or something one of your competitors may do.

Depending on your company, your legal department may understand this and have legal personnel ready to take any of these possibly patentable ideas and process them for patentability. On the other hand, your legal team may know nothing about patents and patentability and completely rely on Outside Counsel (or OC) for the review and processing of ideas. Either way, you need to prepare your legal department for the possible generation of patentable ideas and determine the process you will take when they are generated. Please see the patentability chapter later in the book to determine if the idea in question should go to the legal department for review. Experience will tell you when an idea is patentable immediately. Until you get there, please rely on your legal team or the guidelines in Chapter 6.

Inventors

These are your idea generators.

Who is an inventor? Anyone within your organization that you would like to solicit ideas from. Ideally, IMHO, this is enterprise-wide, but in some organizations, you may need to restrict it to a smaller group. In one organization, a major retailer we worked with, while it would have been ideal to extend it to the entire organization (which at the time had 2M global employees), we kept it to the ecommerce group only, of which there were about 3000 employees at the time. As mentioned above, you may have to restrict it to full-time employees only, which will require that your technologists program the system in such a way as to only allow full-time employees into the system. Even if you can do that, sometimes some names sneak in, and you may have to discard some ideas if a contractor or two gets into the system (this happened to us a few times, and it was unfortunate as the ideas they had come up with were pretty good – but we couldn't legally reveal that.

Beyond selecting who will submit ideas, which we suggest is everyone, you will also need to decide if you wish to allow for anonymous submissions. While these are not truly anonymous, since the login system will likely know the identity of the submitter, this may provide a layer of comfort for inventors with truly radical ideas to allow them to come forth. It really depends on the culture of your organization – some organizations will not allow it, others may believe that those are the best submissions, as the inventors are free to disconnect themselves from the idea, and therefore pose very disruptive and challenging ideas.

As mentioned earlier, in one session, someone once posted

anonymously that "half of the middle management team should be fired as non-essential." We had to initially block the name of the submitter from the CEO until he relented and agreed that whoever posted that should remain anonymous (along with the hundreds of voters who upvoted the idea too.)

Your inventors are your lifeblood. Without your inventors your program will fail miserably, so make sure that you take very, very good care of your inventors. Some tips:

- Communicate, communicate, communicate and again, communicate

- Never let them think that their ideas have fallen into a black hole

- Respond quickly to all queries, even if you must tell them that you are still working on reviewing them

- Once you know the disposition of an idea, let your inventor know immediately what will be happening to the idea, even if you won't be moving forward with it. Not knowing is worse than hearing someone say "no" quickly

- Provide feedback via the crowd. Don't let yourself or your team be the only responders. Build a system to allow the crowd to review and vote on the ideas

- No one or no idea left behind. Decide on the disposition of every idea, and let the inventors know as soon as possible what will happen to them

- Recognize their contributions to the program in some way. Hook their stats in with HR and let them know how many ideas, votes, and reviews they contributed. Make engagement in the program part of their KPIs. Bring the top inventors onto the stage at the monthly or quarterly all-hands meeting and let them talk about their ideas. Award the top inventors with lunch with the president, a ball game in the corporate box, a monetary award (typically for filed patentable ideas only) or just plain old very public enterprise wide attaboys and pats on the back.

Reviewers

These are also your inventors, but they can also be handpicked teams who review the ideas in stages.

Ideally, you should set up a program where anyone can invent, and anyone can upvote or downvote any idea, as well as drop a review against the idea.

As the ideas are collected, you can set up timebox stages where you collect ideas, then vote on ideas, then review ideas, through different stages and by different teams.

For example, here is a set of possible stages

1. Idea submission
2. Idea voting
3. Idea review – Management Team
4. Idea Review – Technology Team
5. Idea Review – Legal Team
6. Idea Decision
    a. Move Forward with Prototype
    b. Move Forward with Patent
    c. Move Forward with both Patent and Prototype

    d. Needs more information

    e. Do not move forward currently

This is just one model. We can't dictate which model will work best for you, as every corporate culture is different. We've run programs with specific time-boxed stages like the above, and others where there was a complete free-for-all, and anyone could do any of the above steps 2-6 in any order, once the idea was submitted.

In that case, anyone could vote, comment and review on any idea once it was submitted, and the teams could pick an idea out of the system to prototype and patent at any time. It was a little chaotic, but it worked for that company.

We seem to keep returning to culture fit, as it is the main thing that I kept coming across in companies with both successful and unsuccessful programs. The closer your program fits with the corporate culture, the more successful it will be.

Approvers

These are usually your senior managers, the folks who can pluck an idea out of the stream, depending on the process, and move it to prototype, patent, or even direct to product in rare cases. We usually use a cross-functional team as approvers, with the team recommending to senior management which of the selected ideas should be greenlighted.

When it comes to funding the greenlighted ideas, the funding can come from many sources, but typically your executive sponsor can step in at this time and find a place for the ideas within the organization.

A Note on External Programs

While this book is focused on internal crowdsourced innovation programs, you may wish to run an externally focused program, which includes prospects and customers. Examples of these include My Starbucks Idea and LEGO Ideas where your inventors and reviewers are not your employees. While these programs are great, they are out of scope for this book, as they require a completely different set of legal requirements (even though you can use the same technology to run them). If you wish to run a program like this, you will need to involve your market research folks, who are already quite adept at talking to your customers, your legal team and your marketing people. You will need to have your inventors and reviewers give up their rights to the idea once they have submitted it, and you can't provide any guarantee that the ideas submitted, even if they are awesome and your customer love them and upvote the hell out of them, will ever come to light.

Additionally, your customer may also use this as an alternative communications channel to discuss (and or complain) about your company, its people or its product. Either way, external programs have a whole other set of challenges, when done right are amazing. But check with those teams mentioned above if you would like to run an external program.

CHAPTER 4

WHAT'S THE UPSIDE?

I was at an innovation outpost event (companies not based in Silicon Valley have innovation "outposts" here so that they can breathe in the heady vapors of the innovation brewing here) when the presenter made a very interesting remark. That remark stayed with me, and now I seem to be hearing references to it over and over, with regards to the expected outcome of an enterprise innovation program, which I've blogged about before. I think that he made up the remark on the fly, during his talk, and at first, I thought he was being facetious, but as I hear more and more people use it, I'm thinking that may not be the case.

That remark was:

"It's not innovation unless it's a billion-dollar business."

He was referring, I thought jokingly, to the output of an internal innovation initiative. A billion-dollar business, otherwise known as a "unicorn, " is called that simply because its typically rare, although if you read the startup news, seems like there's a new one born every minute, and they are being born faster and faster. Of the last few unicorns, (the prescription discount site GoodRx among them) some made it to billion-dollar status within four months! But that's the startup world.

So, I thought, that can't be true. The very next day I was attending a webinar where they were presenting the results of an internal, enterprise wide crowdsourced innovation program at a very large prestigious financial enterprise which shall remain nameless. As they were going through how the program was being set up and what the theme and the communications of the program was like, they talked a bit about how the CEO presented the program. He gave a rousing speech, but then capped it off with "We are depending on YOU to come up with our next **billion-dollar business**." I thought, OK, maybe he was being aspirational, setting sights high is great. Since then I've heard it twice more! CEOs and CINOs kicking off innovation programs by asking for their employees to deliver unicorns.

I wondered, what if they don't? Will, they shut the programs down? Is $100M not good enough? Or even $250M. Does it have to be a unicorn to interest the C-Suite? Is it true? It sounds like leaders of enterprises are now looking at those companies and using that as a yardstick for the success (or failure) of their internal innovation initiatives. Are they expecting unicorns?

Like a VC, it looks like even large enterprises think that innovation needs to be insanely profitable (although not particularly massively huge, game changing or disruptive since that may be a threat to the business) – even enterprise leaders want unicorns to call their own. (Why not, they are so cute, aren't they?)

In all seriousness, if the yardstick of success for an innovation program is a nothing less than a billion-dollar business, then what kinds of innovation are we going to see? If we only look at the pure bottom line, how are we going to get out from under the "how can we make things way more profitable?" mindset. Sure, the business of business is to make money – however, if you focus on that above all, who knows what amazing innovations you are going to leave on the table. Who knows what the downside is of tossing incremental products, process improvements, and other micro innovations because they are too small. A thousand incremental innovations could lead to multiple unicorns, but if you only go for hitting it out of the ballpark, you'll forget that base hits and walks count too.

Sure – set your sights high. But don't expect every idea to be a hit. You'll probably never know which one will. Like a good VC, place a lot of small bets, and if you get lucky, and let your people be as innovative as they can be, then the home runs will come. While there are immeasurable benefits which can you can from your innovation program, aside from the possibility of building a new business up to and including a billion dollar one (if you are very lucky)

That's the upside for the business. What the upside for the employee? What's in it for them? In this chapter, we'll explore the various incentive programs that you can use to help employees get their ideas out of their heads and into the system.

There are as many flavors of incentives as there are companies out there. What works will be, as mentioned before, something that works for your culture. Let's delve into a few we've seen out there; just a tip, the most effective are not necessarily the most expensive.

Before we start, some people think you need to give people amazing incentives to give up their best ideas because they think that if the idea was good, your typical employee won't give it up. They think that the employee might want to keep the idea to themselves because they may one day wish to leave and start a startup to implement the idea.

That is a false assumption. Your employees are your employees because they prefer being your employees, and not startup entrepreneurs. If they wanted to be startup entrepreneurs, then they probably would have gone off and already become startup entrepreneurs. Those who are still your employees and have good ideas, they may not be interested in that risk, and therefore stay with you. However, they still love their ideas, so giving them to you to implement is their way of telling you that they trust you with their precious ideas. So, you better treat those ideas (and their inventors) well.

Prizes, whee!

Back in Toronto where I'm from, we have a city fair which takes place every year and ends in September just before school starts. I remember going down there as a kid every year – it was a ritual for my family, and then later as a teenager, with my friends, to go down to the Canadian National Exhibition. It's one of those fairs which has been going on forever (Wikipedia says since 1879!) – I'm sure that when it started it was agrarian and has since morphed into a yearly fair which features all kinds of food from all over the world, rides (roller coasters, Ferris wheels, one year they had bungee jumping) and of course, games. They had everything from those tossing games (rings, balls, coins) to shooting games, which were my personal favorite. Not sure why, but I was really good at those shooting games – you know the ones where they have a fake rifle mounted on a bracket in front of you on a little gimbal, and you could rotate it slightly to try to pinpoint the target, which if I recall looked a bit like a set of teeth you could shoot down. You had to shoot the middle short tooth down to get the big prize. Even though they messed up the sights to attempt to screw people who really knew how to shoot weapons, for some reason I was good at sighting the first shot, figuring out how they had messed up the sight, compensating, then bagging the big prize on the next shot, which was usually a big stuffed toy or something. I get the allure of prizes

Prizes are cool at the fair, but, IMHO, not so much for your inventors. A tech company we had engaged with thought that giving away iPads for the top inventors was a great idea, unfortunately, most everyone already had an iPad. Gear the prize to what appeals to your inventors.

If you are keen on offering a prize, it's key to pick something that would be a real treat for the inventors. It doesn't even need to have anything to do with innovation – it could just be box seats at your local teams sporting event, or tickets to a local museum or a modern art event. We've found that specific physical items which are thought of as being of value, don't cut it. You end up spending a lot of money for the prizes and may not get the return you expect.

Experiences

Experiences are great prizes, effective and may not be that costly:

1. Local museums, galleries or special events

2. Trips to other offices within your company with no expectation of anything other than interacting with people from that other office

3. Trips to any external innovation centers you may have

4. Attending an innovation or foresight conference

5. Let your employees work as a "nomad" for a week – moving from co-working space to coffee shop to home and about.

However, none of the above should happen with any expectation of a return – don't expect them to come back with a report of the state of innovation in your Barcelona office or anything like that.

We are big believers in serendipity. As you will see in the one of the exercises we have at the end of this book, you should foster serendipity by allowing your employees to do, be and experience something different. One of your awards could be just that.

Cash

For regular idea generation, cash awards fall into the same kind of category as prizes. Money motivates some people and they will generate ideas to augment their income. It sometimes becomes an issue when you have a patent awards program, which is beyond the scope of this book but should be a component of every innovation program, which we'll talk about later. Cash may also be a bad idea from a compensation standpoint –your HR team may have a concern, as would Uncle Sam, Sven, Saul or whoever your taxman is named after. So, cash is not recommended, at least for regular innovation program rewards.

When it comes to patent awards, however, it is standard across the industry to offer a patent award to one or more named inventors on a patent. Typically, it is a two-part award, which is a different amount based on how many inventors there are on a patent. It's best to consult a patent attorney on this, however as an example, here is one of the programs I was a part of:

Single Inventor

1. $2000 on filing. As it is on filing, the idea must be good enough to file, the patent attorneys or your patent review council will determine if it is suitable.

2. $2000 on issuance (typically 4-5 years after filing and only if issued)

Multiple Inventors

1. $4000 split among the inventors at filing

2. $4000 split among remaining inventors at issuance

This is one of the richer programs. However, there are many, many ways to run a program like this – sometimes it a much lower number per award, sometimes it's more if you have the same inventor coming back with more and more great ideas. Consult with your corporate patent office or attorney and see if they have any ideas. If not, there is always Google, or you can contact us, and we can help you with setting one up which would be appropriate for your budget.

Access

This is one that always works extremely well. This "prize" is giving your winning inventors unfettered access to your senior management, in something like a lunch or a pitch. What we've done with a lot of success is a "Lunch with the CEO," where the winning inventor or team attend a private lunch with the CEO of your company to discuss the future, not to necessarily pitch the idea. Access works in different ways, depending on how typically accessible your CEO is to the rest of the company. Your winning inventors would love to be able to have a sit down with the boss. A nice, quiet lunch, maybe something in their office, catered, and hopefully with a whiteboard, or even at a local restaurant where they can chat in peace.

If the CEO is not available, you can easily select someone else in the C-Suite who is high up and may seem inaccessible.

You can also tie the access to the kind of challenge you are running. For example, if you are running a challenge to talk about ways in which your companies' network might be compromised, then a sit-down with the Chief Security Officer might be good, as would a "develop new product challenge" might be to a CMO or Chief Sales Officer. Use your judgement, ask some inventors before you pick the prize – ask them – "Hey, wouldn't it be cool if you had lunch with X as a prize?" If they agree, then you are good.

Best for last.

Recognition

Of all the methods we've used to trigger and assist in engagement for any program, be it a small hackathon to an enterprise wide crowdsourced program, the best and most effective (and possibly the cheapest) way to do it is to offer recognition of the inventor (or inventors) to the rest of the company. Not external recognition, which is great, but usually very high-level internal recognition works great. Here are some of the ways we have recognized inventors

1. During all hands meetings, pull the inventors who won the last challenge onstage and tell them what a great job they did inventing their idea. It's up to you if you decide to put them on the spot to talk about it or give them kudos for it. Best if kudos come from the CEO very publicly

2. Send out an internal communication to your company featuring the inventors

3. Have a real or virtual "hall of fame" – with "inventors of the quarter," "inventors of the year" etc.

4. Shoot a video of your inventors talking about their ideas and post it online on your intranet

5. Hold an "Innovation Day" where your inventor teams can pitch the idea to other employees, Shark Tank style, and have the crowd vote for the best one. Videotape the entire thing and put it on your corporate network.

In my experience, recognition is a very powerful driver of innovation. It must be very public and enterprise wide recognition. Imagine if one of your employees in some obscure department comes up with an idea which may (or may not) be your company's next unicorn, and is then presented to the rest of the company as a great inventor whose ideas are being heard? Can you imagine the overwhelming sense of motivation that will hold for the entire company – that anyone, anywhere internally can innovate to such a level to be recognized by the CEO. Now that's powerful.

CHAPTER 5

END RESULTS

The party's over – what do you do next?

In the example I gave at the beginning of Chapter 2, our hapless innovation lab director was caught off guard by the lack of response or recognition of the awesomeness of the labs work when he tried to move these fantastic new products that were envisioned by the lab, into actual production. Even though he had created some amazing new products, some of which might have been unicorns if they have been built and launched, the company's IT department was nonplussed. If you look at it from their perspective, you can completely see why it went over so poorly: they probably didn't have the people or the budget to take on building the product into something. Even though everyone on the "innovation" side thought that it was a great idea, there was no one on the other side, ready willing and able to take it on. Even if it didn't have the added weight of having to be completely re-written from scratch, it would still have been tough to productize the idea.

As you are planning the outcomes of your innovation program – if productizing the ideas coming out of the program, its key to have a place for these ideas to land so that they can be productized. They need to have people, place, and budget so that they can go-to market. Otherwise, you won't be successful. Idea after ideas will hit the brick wall and never go anywhere, and your inventors will start becoming unhappy about where their ideas end up and maybe even stop submitting ideas completely. I've seen this way too many times: where does the idea go once it's got legs?

You've got some great ideas from your inventors. They got a lot of votes. Your reviewers thought that they were great. Your approvers gave them a big thumb up. Now what?

Prototype

Depending if you are running an innovation program or hackathon which is supposed to end with a prototype (such as a lab or a traditional hackathon) or not (this is more for those who are not) then the next stage in the process would be to prototype the idea. This can be done in several different ways.

1. You can have a few dedicated coders who can take the idea and turn it into reality. In some cases, you will have some people who can be dedicated to developing prototypes on your team – that's the absolute best solution. In that case, you would add these folks to your team. At minimum, you need a front-end developer and designer who can develop a very compelling front end for your prototype, as well as a back-end developer who can do the back end or functional parts of the prototype

2. These same people could be on a different team, and you could "borrow" them for a short period to develop a prototype

3. There may be a roving team of developers out there who could be freed up to work on your prototypes as they become available.

4. You could outsource the idea to a company like Gigster or a small external development team. Take care here as this is your new IP and you (and your lawyers) may not wish it to leave your premises.

5. The inventors of the idea, as they are likely very passionate about it, may help you build the prototype if they either have the skill set to perform some of the tasks required or can at least pull in some of their other team members to help. This works great if you have a company which has some "free time" rules (like the Google 20% rule, which allowed employees to work on projects which had no direct connection to their jobs 20% of the time)

Wherever you get the resources, it's important to generate at least a few prototypes of your most promising ideas. I can tell you from experience that a great PowerPoint or Keynote will not have the power of an actual working (and good looking) prototype. I might argue that the prototype must look better than it works. Especially today, you can win hearts and minds with a very well designed (over a highly functional) prototype.

The other great thing about the times we are currently in you can develop a nice working prototype with very little money and time, especially with all the great new frameworks to develop both web and mobile apps out there. It used to take a million dollars and a year to put up a static website. Now a small team can build very sophisticated mobile apps in a few days to a few weeks.

Remember the key reason that you are building a prototype: to convince someone to be able to release the funds and people to make this real. You may even need to throw away all the code, but it doesn't matter. Its sole role is to convince those with the means to support the vision of the prototype.

Product

Sometimes an idea is so amazing, you can convince someone to put it straight into the product pipeline, and it will just move forward on its own. This is great (and rare) when it happens. Again, the chances of something like this occurring depend on the culture of the company. I remember taking great ideas to different groups within one of the companies I was working at and them telling me that they already had an incredibly tall stack of stuff to work on, and they had no time to do anything about the ideas I brought in. They didn't even look at the ideas to determine if some of them were so good that they should reprioritize the stack to fit a few of these in. Other companies may be more open to slotting some new ideas in, especially those with a much more agile management style.

Patent

If you can't get your company to prototype or productize your idea, and you still think it's an awesome idea, and no one else has done it, then you really should file a patent on the idea, just in case you or your competitors wish to build the product in the future. I'll go more into this in the next chapter, but patenting an idea is great for those really good ideas to go if they have never been done before.

Depending on if your company already a patent or patent awards program has, an awards program would be a great incentive for the inventor.

Always Have a Landing Strip

Every idea, no matter how big or small, must always land somewhere. Even if it lands in "NotHappeningVille" you must always let the inventors of each idea what is happening to their idea. Feeling that their ideas are disappearing into black holes is the kiss of death for any innovation program. If you want to keep the ideas flowing out of your inventors, you must keep the flow of feedback and communication about their inventions and the innovation program itself going strong.

CHAPTER 6

WHAT'S PATENTABLE?

Note for this chapter: I'm not a patent attorney, although I do hang around many of them and they are all very nice people — so if you have more detailed questions regarding an actual patent or patentable idea, please consult an attorney. I just like inventing.

Ideas are awesome. Of course, many people have said many things about ideas, like "Ideas are a dime a dozen" or "Execution matters more than the idea itself" but if you ask me, everything starts with an idea. The idea is not good or bad in and of itself; it simply has attributes which can determine where the idea goes in life. An idea can be born anywhere and at any time, and some ideas become great businesses. Other ideas are great enhancements to current existing products; some ideas enhance products so well that they completely transform products into something completely new or refocus products to open completely new markets.

Once you have an idea, what do you do with it? That's my main concern — some people enjoy generating ideas, they never expect to profit from them. Others grab onto an idea and think that it is so amazing that billion-dollar businesses can be built on that idea. Others might think that the idea is so unique and new that even though that they cannot afford that time and/or money at the moment to develop the idea into that billion-dollar business, they at least wish to register the fact that they were not only the first to come up with the idea, they want to be able to do something with the idea eventually, so their first thought is: let's patent it.

As you know, patenting an idea allows you, and only you (or your company), to develop that exact idea into a product or service. It's the same as copyright, however, instead of being for content which can be copied (book, blog, audio, video), it applies to a process, or in some cases a visual design (in the case of a design patent).

There is a common misconception that, like a copyright, if you have an idea and write it all down, then you are protected because you made note of that idea. That used to be the case, (it was known as the First-To-Invent Rule) until President Obama signed the America Invents Act in 2013, which moved us to the more global standard, the First-To-File rule. Under that arrangement, you had to file your idea to "save the date" when you invented it, to be the first to invent it.

Patenting allows you to protect your idea from others who might copy or steal it, if someone does, you have recourse through the legal system to stop them. Additionally, it allows you to license the idea to others for a fee, and you can get a royalty paid to you each time a product is developed. For example, let's say that you came up with a new design for a Bluetooth based speaker system which attached to your shower stall so that you could listen to music in the shower, and it was connected to your smartphone which is within range. You could give the smartphone rudimentary audio commands from the shower to skip to the next song, play again, or play another playlist. Great idea, but you have no idea how to start a company and build these. So, you patent the idea, then once the patent has been granted, you can try to license the idea to a company to develop it for you, and then every time a unit is sold, you get a small percentage in royalty off that unit.

Great idea, eh? Only a few small issues: it takes a relatively long time to have a patent issued (up to 4-5 years from filing – there is another option which is faster and cheaper, called a provisional patent, which lets you protect the idea for a year – just enough time to gather the funds to do a utility patent), there is a cost involved (between $12-15k per filing for the utility patent), and the idea itself needs to be reviewed by examiners at the US Patent Office. They are the ones who can determine if the idea is worthy enough to be granted a patent, and there are typically three specific criteria which they look for to determine patentability.

These criteria are novelty, usefulness, and nonobviousness. In our work, we also add a fourth criteria, visibility, which ensures that if someone is attempting to steal your patent, we can tell.

Novelty

Novelty is typically the first criteria of patentability in our book. Simply put, if you can answer the following questions:

1. Has this ever been done before?

2. Has this ever been thought of (and written down, or described publicly) before?

3. Has this ever been patented before?

All with a firm "No," then you may have a patentable idea on your hands.

Here are some examples of ideas which made it through the novelty filter:

The Post It Note – otherwise known as "Releasable adhesive pads "

Twitter – otherwise known as "Device independent message distribution platform "

One of mine, "Automated Friend Finder, " a system to help people find friends on social networks.

In my opinion, there are a few ways in which ideas are novel. Many people believe that there isn't anything new under the sun, and just like all stories are a variation of Joseph Campbell's Hero's Journey (aka the monomyth), and that everything is built on something that has come before. If this is true, then all ideas, no matter how novel and new, are simply a combination of ideas which came before, put together in new ways. I'd agree that there are many ideas like that.

Take the iPod, an example I've used before. The iPod is a

combination of several ideas, which culminated into a single breakthrough product. There are no less than seven patents on the core features and functionality of the iPod, as can be seen here, but it was Steve Jobs who first put it together in the way he did, and the result is history. Who knew that taking an MP3 player, combining it with a portable hard drive, and wrapping it in a novel user interface would be such a hit?

In that case, look at your idea. Is it a combination of several ideas, put together in new, novel ways, never seen before? If you can answer that question with a yes, it's time to take the idea to your patent attorney. They will do what's known as a "prior art search" to determine if the idea indeed is novel.

Via Wikipedia:

To assess the novelty of an invention, a search through what is called the 'prior art' is usually performed, the term "art" referring to the relevant technical field. A prior art search is generally performed to proving that the invention is "not new" or old.

No search can cover every single publication or use on earth, and therefore cannot prove that an invention is "new." A prior art search may, for instance, be performed using a keyword search of large patent databases, scientific papers and publications, and on any web search engine. However, it is impossible to guarantee the novelty of an invention, even once a patent has been granted, since some obscure little-known publication may have disclosed the claimed invention.

Don't try this at home, kids. Not only are patent attorney's more skilled than you at finding other ideas which are like yours, they also have access to tools you may not have. If you DO this, it may invalidate your idea. Simply seeing other prior art before you take the idea to your patent attorney could "infect" your idea with elements of the prior art, and therefore when you do finally take it to them, not only will you have to disclose that you saw the prior art, your idea may infringe on another and it will be invalidated. If you can help it, don't look at prior art unless it's your firm's policy.

Typically, we prefer that inventors do not do prior art searches on their own. However, it depends on the policies of your company towards patents. If your firm wants you to perform your prior art searches, there are some excellent recommendations at the following sites:

- 5 Crucial Things to Understand About Searching for Prior Art http://www.inc.com/stephen-key/5-crucial-things-to-understand-about-searching-for-prior-art.html

- Should I Do a Prior Art Search? http://store.inventorprise.com/content_articles.php?id=1033

- I Can't Find Prior Art for My Invention http://www.ipwatchdog.com/2013/12/14/prior-art-for-my-invention/id=46793/

- Five Easy Prior Art Search Tips You Need to Keep in Mind https://www.innography.com/blog/post/five-easy-prior-art-search-tips-you-need-to-keep-in-mind

- Patent Prior Art Search Guide http://www.uspto.gov/patent/initiatives/prior-art-search

If you do come up with something like your idea, there is still hope. You will still have to disclose that you saw the previously filed or patented idea, but if you can give your idea a brand-new twist, by adding something else new and different, it may pass the novelty filter after all. But that's not all; there are three more filters to go.

Non-Obviousness

This is a fun one. Many times, people come to me with ideas which are slightly better than something out there and ask, "Is this patentable." Of course, after novelty (can you say that what you are doing is new), the next gate that you must get through is non-obviousness. My definition of that is "can we say that your idea is simply an extension of another idea?" Here are some examples of obviousness, maybe you can spot the pattern:

Making something larger or smaller. For a real-life example, look at the iPhone and the iPad. The iPad, while some call it innovative – is it patentable under the non-obviousness criteria? Not in my mind, since its simply, really, just a larger iPhone. It shares most of its components with the iPhone, and apart from the size, and the lack of cellular voice capability, it's the same device

Swapping one thing out for another which could conceivably be used for that purpose, without adding additional differentiating features. Replace a car steering wheel with a joystick? Or handlebars? Or foot pedals? Probably misses the non-obvious boat. Using brainwaves? That's not obvious. Maybe that's patentable

Taking the same thing which works in one space and doing it in another. May be a great idea or a good business, but patentable? For example, Uber for Flowers? Yo for Pizza? AirBnB for cooking? This one is a little trickier because in many cases you do have to change the model a lot for it to work, and in some cases, you will add that new component, while you are changing the model, which will make it non-obviousness. For example, let's say "Yo for Pizza" – this is obvious, because Yo is a communications tool between people, and one of those people happens to now be a pizza place. Or Magic, that service that gets you anything you want, within reason, via text. May be a great business idea, but patentable based on nonobviousness, not in my opinion. Say Uber for Flowers is delivering flowers on demand from hobbyist florists on demand – the only difference is that the delivery is from a non-florist. A lot of the sharing economy, gig economy businesses are likely not patentable in their business model. However, the algorithms that run them may be. We'll cover that later with "visibility."

Is your idea an obvious extension of something already out there? There are plenty of patentable ideas which are mashups of more than one idea, which is great. If, however, you are taking an idea which is already out there, and simply adding a small variation which the original inventor may not have thought of the first time around, well that probably fails the non-obvious test.

The inventive step and non-obviousness reflect a general patentability requirement present in most patent laws, according to which an invention should be sufficiently inventive—i.e., non-obvious—to be patented. [1] In other words, "[the] nonobviousness principle asks whether the invention is an adequate distance beyond or above the state of the art."

Usefulness

This one is an easy one. Take one look at the invention and ask yourself, "Is this useful?". There are many, many cool ideas, but if they are not useful, then they probably don't qualify as a patentable invention.

For example, an artist creates a hammer made of glass. The moment you use the hammer to attempt to hit a nail, the glass shatters. Interesting idea, not useful. Now take that same idea but use a brand-new glass formula which is stronger than cast aluminum or steel and just as tensile. The resulting hammer is super light, and surprisingly can hammer nails more effectively than a normal hammer, due to the new properties of this glass. Is this patentable on the grounds of usefulness? Heck, yes.

Now remember that "usefulness" is not a good or bad thing, and it has nothing to do with if something is legal or illegal, or culturally frowned upon, or may be embarrassing or weird, or is something you figure could never possibly come to pass, since there are probably laws or regulations against it. When we patent, we forget about all that stuff – we don't care if it should be done, we only care if it can be done. Some companies will decline to patent ideas unless they are useful to themselves or their customers, either today or in their future. For example, if you work for a bank and come up with an awesome new food source, they may not patent the idea as they think that they will never get into that business, no matter what happens in future so that that idea won't get patented through their program. If you still want to go ahead with the idea, before you disclose it to anyone, consult your employment agreement and you companies legal counsel. Typically, once you join a company, any ideas you come up with may become theirs automatically, so check your agreements.

When you think about "usefulness," it's entirely possible that you may come up with an idea that has a negative impact on some people but is useful to others. Say for example you come up with a tool to manage renters by watching their every move via some internet of things device you install in their apartments. While the renter might hate the idea, the building owner might find it useful. By that criteria, it could be a patentable idea.

Visibility

This is the final criteria that we use with all our clients. It's not something that the patent office cares about, but you probably should. Visibility is the ability for your company to detect if someone else is infringing upon your patent.

For example, let's say that you patent a new way to display search results based on some super sophisticated algorithm. You patent the algorithm and put it on your site. A few months later, your competitor is showing the same results. You assume that they have stolen your algorithm and move against them legally. They disclose the algorithm that they use and its completely different from yours, but in some cases, produces the same results. Since neither of you had any visibility into the algorithm which produced the results, there was no way of knowing if the algorithm had been stolen, thus causing all manner of legal fees, etc.

However, let's say that you patent a specific way of doing ridesharing, and it's obvious that another company is doing it in the same way.

In that case, the similarities are stark and visible, and you may have a case against that company.

Of course, nothing is stopping you or your competitors from patenting all sorts of invisible stuff. However, one of the reasons you patent ideas is to stop others from stealing your idea, if you can't tell if they have, then that reason doesn't account for much.

In the first example, it was just as possible that the second company HAD stolen the algorithm and the first company was perfectly within its rights to sue the second company and demand recompense and licensing fees. There was just no way to know unless action is taken. With a visible patent, you can easily tell it's been stolen.

Once again, I'm not a patent attorney, so if you have more detailed questions regarding an actual patent or patentable idea, please consult an attorney.

CHAPTER 7

SIDE EFFECTS

Doctor: "I'm afraid the patient is terminal. There is a cure. However, it has some serious side effects."

Patient: "I'll take it! What are the side effects?"

Doctor: "Well, mainly cultural change. All those well-formed hierarchies and communications channels might break down. People might talk to each other, and there might be cross-functional communication. People may decide to spend some of their time thinking about the future of the company instead of doing their immediate jobs and may come up with creative new ways of doing business or new products. You might change so much that you'll be a completely new company."

Patient: "Hmm. Well, I'll think about it."

Change

Back before I moved to the San Francisco Bay Area, there were two magazines that I read on a regular basis: Wired and Forbes ASAP. I would go to my local bookstore (which was named This Ain't the Rosedale Library, which was typically full of communist manifestos and other fringe opinion, but also a big selection of magazines from all over. They even distributed my 'zine for a time which I produced in high school, "OX" – but I digress) and pick those up regularly. I read both from cover to cover, devouring everything new and tech. Living in Toronto, we didn't get that much exposure to the absolute latest and greatest, so when these magazines reported on "what's next" I eagerly ate them up.

Then one day, an issue of Forbes ASAP showed up with the following article in it. Resilience Vs. Anticipation. The cover showed a shot of the US from Earth, and it was boldly emblazoned with "How the West Kicked Butt." I read it cover to cover and by the end, I said to myself "Go West, Young Man." I had to get to California.

What was so powerful about that article? Why did that message send me 2636 miles (4239 kilometers) westward to what some call The Innovation Capital of the World? (Well, I might be the only one who calls it that.) The TL; DR version:

- the East anticipates: they know that they will have snow in the winter and heat in the summer and they plan things out – they anticipate, and careful planning is prized

- the West never knows when they will have the next devastating earthquake, so planning is worthless. Resilience is what is prized – bouncing back from adversity.

So in the nutshell, this is why the West kicked butt – when it prized resilience over anticipation – it made an implicit choice to embrace change, not fear it.

Life is change. There may be stretches where things seem to be static – and elicit mini-tomes like The Great Stagnation (note that Dr. Cowen is from the east coast, not that there is anything wrong with that) but things are always changing, moving – if not visibly, invisibly, out of sight. Innovation is happening everywhere, all the time.

We are in an era of great change. The last 100 plus years have seen more change in the technology, and the culture of the world than the world has seen in the previous thousand. How can you possibly plan or anticipate anything when something can be disrupted in a matter of hours, days or months by an upstart startup who can eat your lunch? You could have a phenomenal idea, executed just slightly incorrectly and bam, you are the Meerkat to Periscope.

Ten years ago, no one had a smartphone with the capabilities ours do in their pocket. Now we are cyborgs, lost without our always on connections. In ten years', time, who is to say that we haven't started to evolve into a new species of human, or spend a lot of our time in virtual reality, only needing to step out to eat and use the bathroom?

With one of these, you won't even need to drop off the net to exercise.

How do you survive all this? The same way companies in Silicon Valley have always survived: build your resilience. Not only does it help you to surf the waves of change which are coming at us, it helps you innovate. Build your company to embrace change, and it will be stronger for it.

The problem is: too many companies live on planning. They plan their work, and they work their plan, and if the plan goes awry, because some unexpected act takes place, then they are screwed.

Innovation programs, innovation labs and hackathons, all do several things, some obvious, some not so obvious. On the surface, they are there to elicit interesting new ideas from inventors internal to your company. For some, it's the source of new unicorns. For others, it's a motivational tool. Or any of the outcomes I described in Chapter 1. But if you want your program or lab or hackathon to be successful, you must dig deeper. You must look at the side effects, which are mostly in culture change.

At that same innovation outposts meetup, the presenter was discussing how some companies come to Silicon Valley, stay for a while, get energized by the innovation, then go back to their home companies or countries, but nothing ever really changes.

Sometimes coming here is like a boondoggle, other times it's like a reward, but if these companies really want to change, to be more innovative, to live truly and breathe innovation as we do here, then they need to be open to change, some of it even radical change, in all aspects of the organization. This is not just product innovation, but service innovation, business model innovation, and even organizational structure innovation. Companies here are experimenting and playing with every aspect of doing business - trying new models, seeing what works better, and adjusting and changing to be more effective.

If you think about it, it's a bit like Agile software development. If you aren't familiar with Agile, it's a way of running a software project in a highly iterative way – there is very little light planning up front, but then you jump straight into code and churning out revisions of the software and showing it to your customers and continually iterating on the design. The former ways to develop software required detailed specifications and then code, and by the time the code was delivered, the requirements changed, and the code had to be changed again. It was a slow and painful process (although some may argue that Agile is a fast and painful process ;)). But its basic underlying tenet was "plan your work and then work your plan" which doesn't mimic the real world.

Well, it may have mimicked the real world in the past, these days, when the fast eats the slow, assuming that "change happens" and that we should embrace it instead of fighting it, will lead us to a better future.

My last questions to you on this topic:

1. Is your organization ready, willing and able to adopt a "change" mindset, that they are willing to change, adapt, in any way to meet future challenges?

2. That the side effects which come out of an innovation program, innovation lab, a hackathon, an innovation outpost or even an extended visit to a place like Silicon Valley may even be more important to your company than any possible businesses that they generate (billion-dollar or not)

3. Are you willing to truly be open to innovations in products, services, and business models?

CHAPTER 8

TO DISRUPT, OR NOT TO DISRUPT

Let's face it – most people don't like change. We like things being the way they are – even the word "upset" has a negative connection – to turn over the "set" to break with the established order. The only problem is – there are so many things we can SOLVE if only we would be willing to "upset" things.

As I write this, I can hear raindrops on my roof – California is finally getting some much-needed rain. We've been in severe drought for over four years now, no doubt you have seen those pretty scary photos of lakes simply disappearing – boats in the middle of the lake simply beached. Our water is disappearing – it has barely rained here, and we are feeling the pain. Until the last few days, we've had almost never-ending sunny days for the last four years. No one knows if we will see enough rain this year to take us out of the drought.

I thought about that when I read and watched an interview with a scientist who hadn't showered in 12 years. He used very little water, only washing his hands just prior performing experiments. He had devised a way to stay clean by spraying himself with a mist that he had invented which combined beneficial bacteria which destroyed the bacteria which made him smell, and at the same time, supplemented his skin with other bacteria (from dirt, apparently) which nourished his skin.

He is now selling the stuff, of course. The story and interview were played for disgust – they even had three willing people from their staff try the stuff out and not shower for a week and (not surprisingly) all but one thought it was awful. The article on the topic was interesting – it mentioned that our penchant for bathing was very strong before the rise of Christianity, which linked cleanliness with promiscuity.

Wonder when "cleanliness is next to Godliness" became the norm.

After I read this I thought to myself: this is a great idea. It's the right approach to address the water situation (if showering does make a sizable dent in our water supply). We don't need to be using all the water that we do: why doesn't some enterprising entrepreneur develop a shower based on this scientist's formula? Instead of a shower every morning, we'd step into a fine mist of this stuff, dousing ourselves and killing all the bad bacteria without using up our precious water. I can see the Kickstarter page even now.

However, when I suggested this to people, they thought I was crazy. What? Aren't we supposed to take showers now? It may be "upsetting" but if you think about it – it's the future. No matter what you think of climate change, reducing our water use can only be good. Why not come up with a waterless shower that cleans you with science.

Yuk, right? No, it's the future. It's INNOVATION.

There is a company here in Silicon Valley called Suitable Technologies who have a product called the "Beam Telepresence Robot." To describe it: it looks like a flat screen monitor (about 20 inch) mounted about human height (around 5' 7") on two pillars, connected to a drive unit on the floor which can move the unit around. The screen has speakers, microphones and a video camera for the remote users to see who they are looking at, and the drive unit on the floor has sensors to detect if it's going to bang into walls. The entire unit is controlled remotely over the internet from a laptop. It's supposed to mimic a real live person standing and talking in front of you, the screen presenting the webcam image of the person controlling it. It is a crude from of virtual telepresence, allowing the remote person to move around a space, interact with people and be virtually there. At first, when you see this thing it looks a little freaky, but then you see your buddy Sven from home office accounting on the screen, and you can chat with them and walk down the corridor with them and even walk into meetings. It's like being virtually there.

There is a local organization called the Institute for the Future here in Palo Alto, CA and they have one of these units. They find it to be a very useful tool and an interesting technology, not only for use in telepresence but also to measure reactions to this kind of technology. I've seen them use it to "beam in" remote presenters and others who can't be there for a presentation. After you get over the initial short shock, you completely get it, and it's like the person it standing right there.

A while back, as an experiment, one of their researchers and someone driving the Beam Pro drove/walked around the corner to a local pub just around the corner of their offices. The moment they came in the door they were, apparently rudely rebuffed and told to leave.

I can't imagine what was so scary about a woman and her telepresence robot. But the clientele was quite agitated, and they asked her and her remote companion to leave. And this is in the heart of Silicon Valley, where we have a shop staffed only by Beam robots. When I thought about this, I realized that the future is very upsetting to some.

Since then, I've seen the Beam robots at the Santa Clara Convention Center. You can rent them if you wish to attend a conference there virtually. No flight or hotel room costs, and good for the environment too.

However, that only makes me think that we are on the mark. If the futures we are weaving, the innovations we are creating aren't upsetting someone, then are we doing our jobs? Are we pushing the envelope? Are we staying in that safe little box when we innovate, or are we making people uncomfortable? Are we upsetting them?

Part of our mandate should be to push the envelope, make people feel a little upset about where things are going. Get them to think about those futures, trigger thinking, trigger innovation, and push them to think thoughts out of the mainstream.

So here is the question: how disruptive can you be when you come up with these ideas in your program? I've mentioned before that some great ideas go unpatented because the company doesn't think that the ideas will have any application in the company's current or future space, and what happens with those ideas which are too upsetting for your company to even think about?

I'm sure that someone, somewhere within your company has probably thought about some ideas which would ruin your company. Products and services are so much better than your own that even thinking of someone out there with them makes your senior people think "let's not go there." I've seen ideas squashed in brainstorming sessions as being too radical (I was in a recent session where someone said – "if we implemented this idea, it would completely undermine our entire industry – might be a bit too radical for us.")

You must think: if my people can come up with an idea like that, then it's likely someone else will as well. That someone else could be your soon-to-be competitor.

So, what do you do?

Optimal marginality

You must find the right balance, based on a ton of factors, but mostly the tolerance of your organization for radical ideas. This is not something I can prescribe – this is something that you will get a gut instinct about how radical the ideas you feel your business can accept.

If you are new to the organization, you probably should tap a more senior member to be on your team, or at least as an advisor, so they can give you a sense for what will and will not work.

Sometimes these things will sort themselves out – when I ran a program for one company I purposely entered an extremely radical idea into the system to gauge the tolerance level. I can't tell you the exact idea, but it had something to do with creating a portal for various religions to present themselves, with information and discussion areas, how to convert to that religion, etc.

That idea was universally downvoted and became the most unpopular idea fast. Even if the commentary against the idea was thoughtful, you could see that the company had no stomach for doing something like that – you could see that it was all risk for little reward. The crowd dissed the idea, giving me a sense of how radical an idea would have to be for it to be knocked down by the company – some slightly fewer radical ideas made it through. By doing that, you get a sense of what's allowed and what's taboo. At least they didn't tell me to remove the idea completely – that would have made it far too radical.

You need to test the boundaries of the disruptive ideas, and slowly push them out. You can't just leap forward and be incredibly radical day one – you need to ease the company towards a more disruptive future slowly.

One of the more interesting exercises I've done is called KILL THE COMPANY. It's a free-for-all brainstorming session where you get people within your organization to come up with ways to disrupt your company into the ground. What would a competitor, or outside agency, or massive change in the industry or the world must do for it to kill your company literally?

For example, let's say that you are a gig economy startup which accepts packages for your customers and holds them at a secure location for them, and then delivers them when they get home. You buy your things and ship them to this service; they text you when the package arrives and then arrange a time for the company to drop it off to your door when you are home. This is a real service which is out there now, BTW. It's mostly for people who are worried about their packages being dropped on their doorstop when they are not home and are then possibly stolen. What could destroy this whole business with one stroke?

FedEx, UPS, and USPS decide to hold the packages at their local location and then text you and ask when to deliver the package, after hours when you are home. One relatively minor revision by a behemoth and your company is toast.

You are the only one who can truly judge the level of disruption that your company can accept. At the same time, it's also up to you to expand that bubble of "safe" ideas to allow your company to grow and welcome those truly disruptive ideas because those are the ones which will truly change your company.

They may even end up as unicorns and make everyone happy.

CHAPTER 9

INVENTOR CARE PROGRAM

In one of the first programs we turned around, every interview we had with an inventor who had submitted an idea into the program had the same complaint

"I submitted my idea, but then it went into a black hole."

We've come across the black hole problem many times, and it is the kiss of death for any innovation program – whether it's enterprise wide or not. Once your inventors get the sense that their ideas are simply disappearing with no timely feedback at all, then they will simply stop giving them to you.

We've never seen a problem of lack of engagement if you give your inventors a place to submit ideas. No matter what the company does, no matter how seemingly ambivalent the employees might be about the company when given an opportunity to voice their ideas, they mostly do so willingly.

Some people suggest that they need be incentivized to do this, but in our experience, employees of large enterprises love to express their ideas on improving things, coming up with new product and services, new ways of doing things to make things better. All they need is a well thought out conduit to allow them to express those ideas.

However, once those ideas have been expressed, the inventor needs to get feedback, and promptly. You don't personally need to give the feedback – but you will, however, need to put some system into place to give feedback. Ideally, you set up the system in a way to crowdsource the feedback as well, turning the program into a kind of perpetual motion machine which runs itself. You may need to incent some engagement at the beginning, or it might just happen on their own. Typically, once you create the environment for submission, voting, and review, and people see and understand it, they will participate.

Communicate Early, Often and Proactively

First things first, make sure that you communicate to your inventors as early and as often as you can. Establish a response time on the idea and make sure that you keep to it. Even if you must tap the idea and give them a "thanks for your submission, we are reviewing it now and will get back to you as soon as possible." Never let them think that the idea went into a black hole.

Initial Idea Submission Perfectly Reasonable Responses for Different Scenarios

1. Thanks for submitting your idea, we've made it available for voting and comment.

   The rest of the company will now be able to review and vote on your idea.

2. Thanks for submitting your idea, but we will not be able to pursue it at this time due to X reason. Ideally, give reasons why the idea won't be pursued.

3. Thanks for submitting your idea, we will forward it to the team that is responsible for those ideas and will get back to you

4. Thanks for submitting your idea. We think that this one may be interesting enough to file a patent on, so we are forwarding it to the legal team for review.

5. Thanks for submitting your idea, we have forwarded it to the prototype development team and are looking forward to their response

6. Thanks for submitting your idea, however, we feel that the idea could use more refinement. (Ideally, specify the refinement level.)

See a pattern here – obviously, you don't need to use the same responses, but do you see what I'm doing? Positive initial feedback for submitting the idea, then disposition.

Unreasonable Responses

1. An autoresponder. As soon as possible, provide a real human response.

2. "We are putting this idea on hold" – nope. If you put it on hold, you may as well tell them that you threw it into the black hole

3. Any other response which might deflate them. Remember that these ideas are their babies – they think of them very, very highly, and if you trounce on their ideas, then be ready for them to shut up.

Sometimes the serial inventors throw out their less than killer ideas out first, to test the waters to see if you are listening and supporting them.

Tell Them What's Going to Happen, Even If It's Going to Be "Nothing"

Don't leave the submitted ideas to sit around for too long. Depending on the duration of the program, whether it's time boxed or continuous, pick a certain amount of time in which to disposition the idea. For example, in a one-month long program, make sure that you disposition the ideas within a month, have at least some feedback and possible actions within a week, and at least some voting and commentary within a day or two. On an ongoing program, at least monthly, gather up the ideas which have not been dispositioned yet and take them yourself to the teams or people who are going to make the decision. Take it to their team meeting or set up your meeting to review and disposition the ideas.

Rewards and Awards

We talked about this earlier, but I stress that when you promise an award, be it a patent award, physical award, recognition or access, don't forget to do it, and do it when you say that you are going to do it. Don't let the CEO keep rescheduling the lunch over and over – commit to a date and stick to it. Make sure that you recognize and celebrate your inventors when you say you will.

Do It Very Publicly Within Your Organization

When you do anything to reward your inventors, make sure that you publicize it within your organization – unless its expressly frowned upon by your legal or HR departments, such as with patent awards. Take the time to talk about what you are doing for your inventors. Use whatever announcement mechanism you have to show off your inventors and their inventions internally. Make sure that everyone knows their names and their inventions. Be very open about the program and how it works and what the good ideas are.

Serial Inventors

Once you start, you may end up with some special individuals who will show up again and again in your system, coming out with great ideas over and over. This is one of the other great upsides of running an internal innovation program; you should be able to determine the inventive individuals in your organization. Once you have identified the serial inventors, try to run some special programs just for them.

For example, if someone submits over ten ideas which make it into the 80% positive and over club, maybe you contact them directly and ask if they'd like to join a special "virtual team" who meets now and then to brainstorm new ideas.

Once you have a good number of these people, run some small 1-2 hour brainstorming sessions and give them a specific challenge that you are facing, and see what they invent.

If you are treating your inventors well, you should treat your serial inventors even better.

In short, take care of your inventors, and you will never be short of great ideas.

CHAPTER 10

THE TECH

This is here because it's not as important as the program itself. The technology that you use to power your program should not be the central focus of the program. The tool that you use to collect, review and vote on the ideas should not drive the process that you use to review and vote on the ideas.

Some program managers may feel that the tool, and maybe the vendor of the tool if they have a professional services arm, will do 90% of what needs to be done to run a successful program. In my experience, the vendor tends to design the program around the tool, since of course, they are trying to sell the tool. It's better to use an independent agency like ours to build the program first, then select the tool that can be set up to implement the program.

We won't list of the tools available because the moment we do that, then this list will be obsolete. However, we can let you know which features should be in base level implementation. Once you are ready to pick a tool, ask your technologist to assist you in the selection of it. You can also google "innovation management software" and see what comes up.

Base Requirements

1. Ability to use single sign on to log in. Leverage your corporate log in. For some smaller companies, a social login, such as Google, Facebook or Twitter can be used. But most likely you will need single-sign-on integration with your corporate system.

2. Ability to show a home page with dashboard with hot news, videos, places the submit your idea and voting on ideas.

3. Ability to submit ideas at varying levels of detail. Key and should map to your goals: if you are looking for a few high-quality ideas, you may want to ask for more information here. If you are looking for more ideas, leave this shorter. At minimum

you want:

    a. Title

    b. Description

    c. Category/Tag or both

    d. File upload

    e. Anonymous or not

4. Ability to notify users when ideas are submitted – both the inventors and the reviewers, voters, and approvers

5. Ability to vote an idea up or down

6. Ability to comment on an idea

7. Ability to attach files to comments

8. Ability to review ideas

9. Ability to change the state of the idea

10. Ability to timebox idea capture, review and disposition phases.

11. Ability to have multiple workflows based on the state or category of an idea

12. Ability to notify teams to review ideas

13. Notifications to keep reviewers, approvers on track and to review and to approve

14. Web and mobile submissions

15. Ability to draft ideas and save drafts before you submit

16. Ability for the administrator to feature ideas and comments on the home page of the tool

17. Ability to give you, the program manager, great visibility into the program metrics. Trust me; you will get asked, repeatedly, "how's the program going?" so it would help you greatly if you could access a dashboard which show you the health of the program every step of the way.

That's the minimum in my view. There are plenty of other features out there as well, and it's up to you to determine if they are important enough to go with them or not. Features like:

1. Gamification: earning badges for doing stuff

2. Markets: people can buy/sell stock in ideas

3. Valuation: get people to guess how much an idea is worth or costs to build

And many others that may overcomplicate the program. If you are starting out – start with as simple a program as possible, then add features only if necessary, and only if your program can take it. I've seen programs go astray when the program manager thinks that they need this cool feature, but then it kills engagement.

Pick the simplest tool which does what you need it to do, then configure it to match your process, and launch it.

CHAPTER 11

THE DEETS

What are the details of the program? What kind of program works best? Did you answer the 5 W's?

Who?

We discussed the people you need to participate in the program and how to engage them in the chapter on people. Are you going to run it across the enterprise, or only for a small group? Is it internal or external? You will need to determine this from the start.

When?

Good question: when will you run it, how long will it be, and will it be phased or continuous? We've run all kinds of programs, and different programs work for different people. Continuous programs need constant communications and upkeep. They are like running a blog – you must keep communicating to keep engagement high. Time boxed programs are good if you want a tightly focused event, you only need to communicate and market the program heavily through the program period, and you still need to communicate after, but it is much less onerous. If you are time boxing, you must decide if you will phase out the program, keeping the different actions against ideas in separate time-boxes (submit, vote, review and approve) or do everything at once. We prefer the continuous, non-time boxed approach, but different things work for different companies. For one company, we ran a continuous program for normal, incremental ideas, and a time boxed month-long program for more disruptive, out-there ideas. You could do the same – for example, running a general continuous program for ideas as your inventors come up with them, and maybe focused time boxed challenges for the others. It's mostly up to you, I may keep talking about this, but cultural fit is again key. Do what feels right for your company.

Where?

For crowdsourced innovation programs, these are typically online. However, you can augment them with in-person brainstorms (we used to do ones before a focused challenge called pre-storms), workshops, hackathons and all sorts of interesting variations. Again, it must work for your company. Physical location typically is not important – but maybe you could use geographic teams and pit them against each other to come up with more ideas.

What?

What will the program be? Small, focused workshops with key personnel or an enterprise wide crowdsourced program across your 200,000 employees? It's all good; it just depends on what feels right for the company.

How?

I think this book answers that one. There are thousands of small details in running a successful innovation program, but here are my key learnings:

1. Get Executive sponsorship
2. Get your team in place
3. Create a cool, fun program
4. Get the software set up
5. Market and launch
6. Communicate like crazy
7. Take good care of your inventors.

One last thing we forgot to do: what kind of ideas should your inventors invent? That's the topic of the next chapter.

CHAPTER 12

UP TO THE CHALLENGE

The first time we rebooted a crowdsourced innovation program, the program that was running was what we would call "challenge heavy" – the software didn't give you the ability to submit any interesting idea, no matter what it was (even unicorns!) unless it was the answer to challenge.

"Challenge" in innovation program parlance, is the problem that your employees are trying to solve with the ideas that they are submitting. It pushes your inventors to think about specific problems and try to come up with solutions for those problems, thus guiding your employees to specific kinds of solutions.

When we rebooted the program, it was "challenge free" – inventors could submit any ideas they would like – we had a rough set of categories and tags they could add to the idea like "cost saving" or "music" or "email" or if they applied to specific corporate units "shipping", "accounting", "marketing", but there was no specific challenge set forth. In my view, that was one of the reasons that the program was so successful; it set our employees minds free to invent whatever they liked. This was for the continuous general program. We later added focused events to work on specific activities, and then simply created new categories in the same tool to track them. For example, in one focused pre-storm, the groups were tasked to come up with new ways to charge for new services. We added a new category called "Paid Services" and held a pre-storm, which then led to hundreds of new ideas in "Paid Services" being added to the tool.

To have or not to have challenges again depends on your corporate culture – although in my view it typically is more indicative of your senior managers view on innovation. Some senior managers feel that if they don't give their employees guidelines, then they will come up with all sorts of crazy ideas which may have nothing to do with any of the problems that they are having. On the flipside, I think it's very useful to give your employees at least the space to come up with out-of-the-box ideas, to spur new thinking. Give them a challenge-free space to start with – let them run a little wild with some crazy new thinking, and then give them some challenges.

Once again, in my experience, this is what works. Your situation may be and probably is, completely different. Try to make sure that your inventors have a space to be free – even if those ideas may not go anywhere within the organization, showing them that there is a place for a little out of the box thinking.

CHAPTER 13

EXERCISES

Now that you have all the information you need to set up your innovation program, here are some tactical exercises that you can use to spur some creative thinking. Feel free to use these or variations of these exercises when you run workshops or any other events.

I've used most of these very successfully in small to large groups, in ideation sessions and in pre-storms, which then led people to enter their ideas into the innovation management software.

This chapter is a collection of 18 exercises that we use to trigger creative thinking – this is just a start, there are plenty more.

Exercise I: Hit Up the Science Fiction Bookshelf

Did you ever do difficult maze puzzles by just going in the opposite direction? I mean its effortless to start at the end and then make your way back to the beginning, isn't it? Sure, you tell me, that's cheating – but you get through the maze, don't you?

Someone high up at an organization I used to work for used to say that thinking about the future is hard. Of course, it's hard – if you start at the beginning – also known as "now."

Luckily, there's plenty of people out there who've given us a clue to where the end is – science fiction authors – they get paid to envision compelling – and sometimes realistic – portraits of the future.

For example, one of the most interesting products I developed – and when we launched this it was before its time, was a retrovisioning of something I read in Samuel R. Delany's Stars in My Pocket Like Grains of Sand. The product envisioned there was called General Information – sort of a just-in-time learning service – when you born you were implanted with a device which instantly answered any question which popped into your head – it was all controlled by orbiting AIs which gave you the answer as soon as you thought it up. Kind of like that scene in the Matrix where Trinity needs to learn how to fly a helicopter in seconds to escape and Tank downloads that knowledge into her avatar. Work backwards from that endpoint, and you have things like Quora and Aardvark (since shuttered by a Google aqui-hire) and one of my patent applications.

If you are looking for new product and service ideas – try the future, then work backwards to today and see if it flies.

One caveat – of course, the future that the author imagined may never become known – or it was wrong – or the market might not be ready for that product (which is what happened to me) – the tough part is not coming up with the ideas – its figuring out if it's too early.

Exercise II: Make Serendipity Your Good Buddy

The Popsicle was invented by enterprising an 11-year-old called Frank Epperson in 1905, who left a glass of soda on his San Francisco front porch with a stirring stick still it. The next day, after a cold night, the drink had frozen. Frank pulled the stick, and, to his surprise, the drink came with it. Nine years later, he patented them as "Popsicles."

If you haven't heard the word serendipity, it's time not only to put it into your lexicon but to live it and breathe it. If you want to be innovative, your culture needs to not only support serendipity but encourage it.

Serendipity: the occurrence and development of events by chance happily or beneficially. "a fortunate stroke of serendipity" Sometimes known as a "happy accident."

Where does innovation come from? Typically, it starts with a problem: someone is having trouble doing something, and there are no solutions, so they put together a solution for that problem, which may or may not be a new, original, innovation.

On the other hand, if you look at several truly breakthrough innovations, they didn't come from someone trying to solve a specific problem. They came out of a mistake, an error, or even more commonly, a juxtaposition of something not commonly juxtaposed. Things not commonly mixed are mixed to come up with something new and different. This is the basis of many innovative new products and services.

How do you foster a culture of innovation via serendipity? Well, first you don't force your employees to come to work, work in the same location, day-in, day-out. You don't keep their noses to the grindstone at their jobs the entire time they are at work. You don't have them sit in endless, repeated meetings.

You encourage them to have a flexible work schedule. You encourage them to have a flexible location. You encourage them to be open to new ideas which can come from any place at any time. You purposely set up an environment and culture where your people can experience new things and new people all the time.

You can't just sit your people in a room and say "Innovate!" Your people need new experiences, new locations, new connections, to build an innovative workforce.

If you asked me today "Chris, I need to start a company with innovation at its core. How would you do it?" this is what I'd say:

1. Don't have an office. I often wonder why anyone has an office at all. A no telecommuting policy, forcing people into an office M-F ends up reducing innovation, instead of increasing it

2. Don't encourage work from home either, encourage work from everywhere. Let your people, no ENCOURAGE your people to work everywhere but in a home office, a coffee shop, the park, a co-working space. But unlike work or school, move from place to place. Move to new physical locations all the time, even during the day – new places mean new connections and new ideas.

3. Have the fewest possible meetings and conference calls – yes you might need a few of these to keep people on track – but after that, leave them alone – are they adults that you can trust, or not?

4. Make your whole company agile, not just your programming methodology. Go back and read my post at thinkfuture.com on Agile Eating the World

5. Use technology like Slack to let people know what's going on. Collaboration doesn't require face-to-face physical connection.

6. Set up a safe place for your employees to report innovative ideas from Day One.

Encourage your people to experience new experiences. Pay for them to go to Burning Man, or Electric Daisy, or SXSW or CES. Let them experience new things, then let them generate new connections and new ideas.

Encourage those happy accidents by strategically placing them in the world and let them roam free. You'd be surprised at what comes back to you.

Exercise III: Get Upset

If something upsets you, does that make it more innovative?

Let's face it – most people don't like change. We like things being the way that they are – even the word "upset" has a negative connection – to turn over the "set" to break with the established order. The only problem is – there are so many things we can SOLVE if only we would be willing to "upset" things.

Remember the stories in Chapter 8 about the "crazy scientist who never showered" or "a robot and a human walked into a bar"?

Part of our mandate should be to push the envelope, make people feel a little upset about where things are going. Get them to think about those futures, trigger thinking, trigger innovation, push them to think thoughts a bit out of the mainstream.

There's so much we could do if we are just willing to be a bit more upset.

Exercise IV: Take the Maze Backwards

When I was young, I used to enjoy doing mazes in paper books. You know the kind I'm talking about – thin or thick newsprint paper books which you can even find today in dollar stores to keep your kids amused on long car trips (if you want to do it the low-tech way and not give them a tablet). I used to spend hours trying to traverse the maze, with my pencil, very carefully starting at the START and making my way to the FINISH, slowly moving down the corridors I thought would take me to my goal. Of course, I'd take wrong turns and need to backtrack, carefully erasing the line I drew with the pencil eraser and taking a different path. I would do puzzle after puzzle like this, taking the wrong paths time after time, probably cursing myself and the maze creator in a fitting childish way.

I'm not sure if I figured it out on my own or some smartass older kid or adult showed me that on the super hard mazes, it was WAY easier to start at the end and make your way to the beginning. Of course, that took all the fun out of it, but it worked, I got through the maze, but it was a cheat. But I got through the maze.

I've always been a big fan of science fiction since I was very young. My favorite show was Star Trek, (the original series). My parents let me watch it even though it wasn't really a kid show – my dad dismissed all science fiction and superheroes (I still remember him watching me watch reruns of Superman flying and him going "People can't fly!". Of course, I was too young to know the term "willing suspension of disbelief, " but I knew that's what I was doing. A very pragmatic guy, my dad.) My mom, on the other hand, liked me watching it because she found that everyone on the Enterprise was always very polite (not sure what other shows she thought people weren't polite on, maybe Kojak?). Anyways, I always loved thinking about the future and wanting to live in that future. Which eventually drew me to Silicon Valley (arguably the innovation capital of the world, as I say on my show) and the field of innovation and foresight.

My love of sci-fi and innovation went together. While others I'd worked with constantly mentioned to me that they thought thinking about the future was hard, I felt that I had a knack for it – that it was easy. Why did I think that? Well, I took sci-fi visions, like Star Trek, and other hard sci-fi authors that I'd been reading, and simply used the "take the maze backwards" trick. I'd read something in one of these novels, maybe set 100 or 300 years from now, and think to myself....

"What's the great-great-great-granddaddy of that? How did that start?"

Start at the end and work your way back. If I read about a subdermal implant inserted at birth which listened to your thoughts and whenever any question popped into your head, it was immediately answered in your head by orbiting AIs which had every answer to every question ready for you, and worked backwards, I might have invented Google and/or Quora before they were born.

Try it yourself. Grab a **hard-sci-fi** novel (not Game of Thrones or any other fantasy – hey we're working now!) and read it. Think about something that they use in the book. Now work backwards through the maze to almost our time, and you may have the next billion-dollar idea.

Exercise V: Waste Some Time

Waste some time for a good cause.

I was reading an excellent article in one of my new favorite magazines, *The New Philosopher*, on Technology. The entire issue was on technology, a great read – you should pick it up.

But I digress. In one article, a researcher had a stunning revelation: he realized that he no longer wasted time. From the moment he woke up to the moment he went to bed, he was always doing something – reading, responding to emails, working out, eating, writing, etc. He noted that he was so busy, that he had every moment of his entire day completely scheduled, and never spent a moment, not even a second, simply doing nothing. He mused: is this what it means to be someone living in the 21st century, an always on, cog in the machine, able to be super productive, every second of every day? I wonder, is this us, now? More than ever before we have the tools, the culture, and the mindset to be ultraproductive all the time, as we are forever hyperconnected into the hive mind.

I'm sure that this is the case for extremely busy people, CEO's and other executives, celebrities, rock stars, and even some of us regular Joe's who might be part of the Shut-In Economy and need someone to do everything for us because Goddammit, we have no time to waste. None.

If you read the prevailing wisdom of LinkedIn, and plenty of other business leading content feeds (you can't call it journalism anymore, can you?) it's all about being more productive:

- 15 Secrets Successful People Know About Productivity
- 10 Timeless Work Habits to Boost Your Productivity Today
- Productivity Hacks: 6 Ways to Fight Distractions

It's all about doing increasingly in less and less time. I even wrote my own 6 Steps to Ultra Productivity. Shame on me – an innovator giving tips on productivity, when, what we need to be innovative is the exact opposite. We need unproductivity. We need to waste time. In the language of that last post – we need distractions to help us innovate, not the other way around.

Focused work is great – when you need to get something done in a short period. Maniacal focus in bursts works great if you have a clear, exact picture of what you are trying to do. But what you need to be innovative is the exact opposite. You need to waste time – to let your mind wander – to walk in curves instead of lines – to make connections you may not have normally made – to let serendipity be your good buddy.

Here is the problem: you probably have some of the busiest people working in your company, typically your top executives. Their lives are so tightly scheduled and productive that they have no time to waste, which gives them no time to innovate – to think about the future – these are the very people who need to be able to have the time to waste to innovate.

If you are one of those CEOs, celebrities, or rock stars, if you realize that you no longer waste time, and you want to come up with new business models, product or service innovations, maybe you need to think about just wasting some time. Who knows what you will invent?

Exercise VI: Go Offline and Make

I love Maker Faire I'm a big fan of the whole Maker movement. Now, it's gone through a few iterations, but I think that the urge to make stuff, to build things, to do things with our hands, is something embedded in our nature as humans. We have this amazing ability to CREATE, but in a lot of us, we haven't had the chance to do it. We used to do it a lot when we were kids, LEGO, Play-Doh, Meccano or Erector Sets. We created all sorts of stuff.

Now I'm lucky, in my role, I get to create, or help others create, nearly every day. There is nothing like the act of creation (although I do remember once some pious fella telling me once that "only God can create" – but I believe we were all built to create.)

We may be wired to create, but the very act of creation takes work. It takes energy. And I find that in day-to-day living, a lot of people have trouble creating because they spend most of their time consuming. It's so EASY to consume! It takes no energy whatsoever – in fact, scrolling through your Facebook stream and tapping a like (and maybe a reaction here and there) is the modern-day equivalent of sitting on the couch, eating bon-bons, and surfing channels. Even that super light touch of liking something is barely a reaction. There is so much that you will never be able to consume everything, and most of the time, the feed that you are getting, are probably irrelevant to you. And if you're subject to FOMO, we'll then forget it – it's an impossible task – you will miss out on something.

How can you find time to create? I read an interesting article in my new favorite magazine, *The New Philosopher*. In this article, they discussed an experiment where they took college students from all over the world and asked them to go offline for 24 hours. No internet, no smartphone, nothing. No access to anything. The reactions ranged from total catatonia – one of the students basically went to bed and stayed there for 24 hours because there was literally "nothing to do" without his connection to the internet, to withdrawal symptoms on par with illegal drug use. Many of the students never made it a whole day – after a few hours, they just had to boot up their phones again. What were these students doing? They were addicted to the connection to others and the consumption of content. While this is probably further evidence that we have now become Homo Nexus, it gave me another idea.

While the researchers in this study had told the students had told the students what not to do "use their phones or connect to the internet" – they hadn't told the student what to do – therefore driving them to give up or enter catatonic state. But what if the researchers had instead said:

Create something.

Draw something, build something, record something, video something or even write something. Just don't get on the internet. Express yourself! Disconnect yourself from the ever-flowing flood of content, good and bad, from every source. Once you've done that – look inside. Look inside yourself for that spark of creativity. That internal flame of creation – of good ideas – unvarnished by the flow of the world into your brain.

You see, your brain has absorbed so much, that now it's time to give back. Stop the flow into your brain and start the flow out of your brain. Try this at home – disconnect yourself from the world and when you feel bored, create. It doesn't matter what it is, make something! I'll bet you won't believe what you will invent.

24 hours later – feel free to get back online and tell the world. But until then, let your brain create.

Exercise VII: Have Beginners Mind

"In the beginner's mind there are many possibilities, but in the expert's, there are few."

When I was in high school I, as probably many others did, found my family's religion a bit wanting and did a little dabbling in several different "ways," spending most of my time reading up on and learning about Zen Buddhism. There was something about Buddhism that I liked, the human centered approach mostly, the idea that you were the focus of your life and followed your own rules, not ones put down by some higher being we may or may not know exists. Additionally, I loved the meditative aspects of Zen, the practice of zazen which has adherents (or aspirants) sit and meditate, clearing your mind of all thoughts, attempting to attain an empty mind, or at least filled with only a single thought or concept, but ideally empty. I even wrote a book, way back when I was in sales, about using zazen to help you chill out when the phone wasn't ringing with orders. (That's right, I wasn't always about disruptive innovation.)

One of the most famous books on the subject "Zen Mind, Beginners Mind" starts out just like the above. Simply with the statement that when someone comes to a practice, any practice, of which they are unfamiliar, the possibilities are endless. It doesn't matter what it is: could be Zen, could be golf, could be snowboarding, could be coding. Your mind is fully open because you have no idea what is right and what is wrong when it comes to the practice. Only when you start learning what to do/what not to do, is when you start closing your mind off to what is not possible. That's when you lose touch with the part of yourself which can lead to disruptive innovation.

Beginners Luck is real. When someone has no rules, no restrictions, on what they are doing, no matter what it is, they make moves and decisions which can create amazing innovations. When you come to something completely new, with no preconceptions whatsoever, you can make breakthroughs in areas people who've done things for years never even imagined. Once you get into it, that's when the rules bog you down, that's when it seems that truly disruptive innovation is out of reach. But it's not.

The fact of the matter is that we can all go back to that moment. We can all "clear our minds" and go back to being a beginner. We can all go back to when we started and bring back that beginner's mind, bring back that childlike curiosity we had when we first started doing something. Bring back that optimistic, sometimes slightly crazy person who started by believing that anything was possible. It is the way back to disruptive innovation.

For some, it may be difficult, but it is possible. Being able to get back to that open state is key to coming up with new ideas.

Exercise VIII: Use the Idea Blender

You may or may not be old enough to remember the old Reese's Peanut Butter cup commercial – they've refreshed it a few times, but if you don't, here it is. They make light of the creation of peanut butter cups by showing one guy walking around the corner eating a giant chocolate bar, and a girl walking around the same corner in the opposite direction eating from a giant peanut butter jar with a giant spoon (yes, apparently walking down the street eating peanut butter from a jar is an common occurrence). Anyways the inevitable happens and bam, they knock into each other, and somehow, the giant chocolate bar ends up in the giant jar of peanut butter – and of course the conversation ensures "Hey you got chocolate in my peanut butter!" and "Hey, you got peanut butter on my chocolate!" said like it's the worst thing in the world. Of course, when they each taste the blend, it is the most awesome sensation ever. "When two great tastes taste great together."

In our workshops, we don't typically knock two people together to see what comes out of it, (unless you'd like us too ;)) but we do try knocking (or blending, more like) two concepts together to see what happens. The best blend comes from taking two completely different things and throwing them together in the idea blender and see what comes out of it. Of course, you don't need to stop at two – you can throw all sorts of stuff in that thing. Think of it like the kale smoothie of innovation – might not look so good at first, but it tastes great and it full of nutrients.

Here's an example

The other day, I was at an ideation session with one of our clients, and someone mentioned that the white board markers smelled like fruit. I'm guessing someone had accidentally bought the wrong kind of markers, so those are the ones that we had (yep Expo Scented Dry Erase Markers), so instead of getting a new set of markers, ignoring them, or just randomly complaining about them, I made those markers the trigger for a whole new set of innovative product ideas. While this is a great example of serendipity being a trigger, blending the idea of the fruity smelling markers with the types of products that the company was trying to build (not fruit or food related in any way) and enabled us to generate a raft of new, completely out of the box ideas, all around smell and color. It unlocked a whole new set of innovative ideas, where we blended their current products with the concept of smell. We even threw some Internet of Things devices and sensors into the blender to fortify our kale shake of innovation. A half hour later, we probably had about 20 new ideas out of that session – some of which were buildable today, others went into the patent pipeline for eventual build out or licensing tomorrow.

It also proves that you need to be open to throwing anything in the blender. Don't stop yourself from throwing something in there because you don't immediately see the benefits of that ingredient. Some of the best tasting shakes have come out of throwing interesting ingredients never mixed before and pressing that smoothie button.

Exercise IX: Face Your Killer

Facing your killer: make it existential

One of the other exercises we use, which we find very rarely used in many companies who have been around for a long time – established, high or consistently profitable companies who don't need to worry about their customers or their product, imagines what, or who would be your killer.

Startups do this all the time: even if they've been able to gain some traction, revenues, and even profit, they are inordinately sensitive to the possibility of another startup, or even another big company, entering their space and completely obliterating the need for them.

Case in point, when Twitter first launched, it created and encouraged a very healthy ecosystem of apps which leveraged their data. I thought, at the time, that they were being forward thinking in that they understood that to become a completely pervasive global communications medium, that they would need to become a platform as quickly as possible. They focused on providing the platform and allowed others to step in and become the interfaces to the platform. It allowed them to grow very quickly – I remember attending their first developer conference back in 2009 when my startup had built a Twitter and Facebook topic harvesting engine called Tweebus. I looked around at the hundreds of developers in the room, all leveraging the Twitter ecosystem to develop applications using Twitter data (as we were) or as new interfaces to Twitter. I say some very interesting innovative new interfaces which I wish were still around today.

A few years later, there was a management shakeup, and Twitter cut off some access, reduced access to others, and hobbled their ecosystem. Many developers lost their businesses completely because they were dependent on the Twitter ecosystem. They died. Twitter was their killer.

Startups are acutely aware of the competition and of the delicate nature of the ecosystem that they play in. In one stroke, you could be worthless.

More mature corporations feel that they are also more resilient. They don't need to worry about their ecosystem collapsing, or that their legions of customers won't suddenly switch to some other competitor. They feel insulated against such stresses.

Welcome to the world of disruption. No one is immune from total collapse from market forces, competitors, and sweeping technological, cultural, and societal changes. Companies deemed "too big to fail" can and will fail. They are more likely to fail since they can never think the unthinkable – that they will fail.

How do you alleviate that? Simply come up with a killer, or combination of them, which will kill your company. What must happen for your company to die? Could it be a competitor? A market crashes? Widespread adoption of Bitcoin? Autonomous vehicles? All or some of the above? Remember, in this world of disruption, anything is possible.

Spend time brainstorming and build the perfect storm of competition, technological, cultural, and social changes which may occur which will crush your company. Start it like this:

If X, Y, Z occur, then our company will die

Spend half the meeting coming up with the above. Once you have that scenario mapped out, let it sink in with your team. On the same day, or a few days later, pull the team together and think about what you would have to do for you to deal with that possibility. How can you address it? What will you need to do/build/be to stay alive in that perfect storm? There you will find innovation.

Exercise X: Kill the Drag

People hate drag – how do you eliminate it?

Just got back from a quick trip to LA and I could not believe how bad the traffic is there. Whenever I needed to get somewhere quickly, people just seemed to be driving like complete imbeciles – straddling lanes, going slowly in the fast lane, dawdling here and there – it was maddening at normal times, and even worse when you are trying to get somewhere quickly. I like to think of this as the concept of drag, which I define as the difference between a customer's seamless ideal experience, and the experience they get. Some people call it friction.

As an example, and the lack thereof, let's look at Uber. Pre-Uber, how did we call a cab? We either stood on a corner and waved one down, never being sure of if or when we would be able to get one, or we called one on the phone, never sure of when it would arrive. Once one showed up, we got in, having no idea what it was like inside, or the quality of the driver. Once inside, not only were we barraged with advertising, we had to trust that the driver was going to take us directly to where we wanted to go, and not take some circuitous route which would rack up the miles to pad their wallets. Once we got where we were going, how much do we tip? Should we tip? The whole process is just fraught with uncertainty. Today, we press a button, a car appears, we get in, it takes us directly to the destination (we can even confirm it ourselves), and at the other end, we get out, automatically paying. Drag is eliminated. Uber is a pure match of supply and demand, with a seamless transactional interface, hiding all the unpleasantries. (As a side benefit, the new huge market of introverts, eat this stuff up)

In some industries, drag makes you money. Who is to say that Google's relevancy isn't slightly off enough to make you page through more pages of their ad imbued site more than others, enticing you to click on an ad? The travel business survives on drag – sometimes I think that the main reason that these sites show you so much information is that they are not interested in getting you the best deal, they want to tire you into picking, something, anything, that's not horrible. But I digress.

However, you may like, or love drag (it may even be your business model) people, in general, hate it. While there may be many browsers out there, when people are ready to make a purchase, typically they want to make it as quickly and seamlessly as possible.

Look at your business: what if you could completely or nearly eliminate drag? How could you devise a set of services which remove all the tiny little, possibly painful processes, which slow your customers down from making a purchase? Or even better, how could you redesign your business model to make life super easy and seamless for your customers.

Here is an example. Do you recall TiVo? I used to have one. At one point they created an interesting innovation – they realized that a lot of their customers had a lot of space on their DVR hard drives, so they created this service called TiVo Suggestions. Like Pandora (or Tinder) you could give 1-3 thumbs up or down on a show, while you were watching it. Over time, not only did it develop a set of likes and dislikes, it automatically recorded shows that you might like for you in the space on your drive. They were set to low priority, so they would automatically be deleted if something you wanted to watch needed the space. TiVo eliminated the drag of finding and recording a show the customer might like.

In the same way, media has now become software and can be delivered at any time and be deleted just as easily. Do you recall when Apple got in big trouble when it pushed a copy of U2s album down to unwitting customers, without asking them? I bet that they wouldn't have gotten any backlash if the "gift" was seamlessly delivered to only U2 fans? Since media is now software, what's the real harm in pre-delivering media that you might be interested in, and then letting you delete it within a period and never get charged?

Think about how your business could reduce or eliminate drag. What can you change about your business model, your purchase process, your delivery mechanisms, to make it simpler and easier for your customers to get the service they want.

Exercise XI: Be Incongruent

To innovate, you must do something different. It's harder than it sounds.

Just read (listened to) Smarter Faster Better, the latest book by Charles Duhigg, the author of the Power of Habit (also another great book). Great book, highly recommended. In one of the chapters, he describes an interesting experiment.

The experiment pulled together a focus group which had neutral views on a topic, say, for example, eating mushrooms (not the example he used in the book). Before the test, they were questioned on the topic to confirm a lack of bias one way or the other.

They were split into two groups: one group was instructed to form a set of reasons for eating mushrooms (health benefits, full of micronutrients) and the other group was instructed to form a set of reasons against eating mushrooms (not vegan, grown in manure). They were given time to create a compelling argument for their case.

They were each able to come up with an extensive list of reasons to support their argument.

At the end of the argument creation process, they were each asked about their personal feelings on the topic. Interestingly, the group that did the pro argument now viewed mushrooms more much more favorably, and the group that did the con argument viewed mushrooms less favorably. Makes sense, right? People were asked to come up with reasons for something, and not only did they justify it for the experiment, they also convinced themselves that they were right.

In the second half of the experiment, each group was asked to do the opposite: now the pro group had to come up with reasons against eating mushrooms, and the con group had to come up with reasons for eating mushrooms. In this, the groups struggled to be able to come up with reasons; both groups were barely able to come up with a fraction of the number of reasons they did earlier.

Once your opinion is set, even in an artificial environment like this, it's hard to change it.

When I heard this, the reasoning came to me. Most humans, except for some in the sociopath space, enjoy being congruent. That their words and deeds align. I voice my opinion on one thing, and even if I see a lot of evidence to the contrary, it's hard for me to change my mind. We feel that it is a very bad thing to change our minds – we rake politicians over the coals for being "flip-floppers," in some cases we take opinions so seriously, that we will defend them at great personal risk, even in the preponderance of evidence against our decisions.

We don't like changing our minds, and we don't like it when people change their minds too often. It is a problem when you are trying to innovate. Innovation requires doing something different – it requires changing your mind and changing your mindset. It requires being incongruent.

Unfortunately, our mind changing muscle has atrophied over time. We tend to make decisions, set directions, make plans, and slavishly stick to them, even if they are not working. It happens to everyone, from managers and employees within mid-market to major corporates, small businesses, and startups. I'm sure you've heard many a tale of startup founders unwilling to pivot to survive because they felt that their original idea was so damn good, all it needed was a little more, time, money or audience and it would have been another billion-dollar business.

Fortunately, however, all is not lost – we can work on our mind-changing muscle, stretch it out, make it more flexible. All we need to do is to open our mind and exercise that mind-changing muscle by making ourselves do new things. For example, decide on a new restaurant for dinner. Order something else you've never done before on the menu. Return something you just bought.

To innovate, we must work to strengthen our incongruency mindset – that we don't always have to do what we say or say what we do. We can, and should, change our minds, our plans, our directions when new information tells us we should. Or even on a whim, as new serendipitous juxtapositions form as we experience life.

So, bend and flex your mind-changing muscle. Now and then be a hypocrite. Argue against yourself. Be the devil's advocate one day, and the angels advocate the other.

Keep your mind nimble and innovate.

Exercise XII: Wander Aimlessly

Do you wonder, as you wander?

It's been proven that rigor and process kill innovation. In one study, two groups of college students were given a problem. But before they had a chance to solve the problem, they made one group walk in straight lines, up and down the room, back and forth, straight lines. Then they told them to solve the problem. The second group was told to wander aimlessly around the room, but specifically not go straight, go in curves, or whatever shapes they'd like. They were then told to sit down and solve the problem. Can you guess which group came up with the more creative solution?

There is a clear difference between creativity and productivity. When you are looking for productivity, you need laser-like focus and straight lines. When you are looking for creativity, you need your mind and your physical body to wander around, both mentally and physically. Wandering around aimlessly triggers completely new thinking – you could make a serendipitous juxtaposition by walking around a corner you've never walked around before, seeing some new view or angle, some stray thoughts and ideas could just flash into your head, jump into the idea blender, and you could come up with something completely new and different.

Lately, there has been a lot of talk on mindfulness and living in the current moment. That we too often think about the future and the next thing, instead of fully realizing everything about where and when we are in the current moment. The strictest practitioners will tell you that you should stop thinking about anything other than the exact thing that you are doing right now, whether its washing the dishes, having a coffee or doing a presentation. While I completely understand where the practice is trying to go, I don't think that pure mindfulness, in a vein of completely emptying your mind of every but that exact thing you are doing, will help you innovate.

What I do agree with, however, is opening your mind to new things. One of the tenets of mindfulness is the extreme opening of the mind to new thoughts, new ideas and new things that can pop into your head.

The human mind is an amazing thing. I often stop and look around at our world and marvel at everything that humanity has invented. Try this the next time, for a moment, when you are at a stop light in your car. Look around you and notice everything around you that humans have created. The car, the traffic light, all the cars around you, the stores, the clothes that people are wearing, everything not natural. Think of all the things that human beings have invented – many of these inventions didn't exist a hundred years ago. Now glance over at your smartphone. Everyone has one, right? Instant interconnectivity to every other human being on the planet who owns one of those, and a vast store of human knowledge, just a tap or a Siri query away. As little as ten years ago, those didn't even exist. The human mind invented that.

Everything innovative, breakthrough and disruptive has an element of randomness within it. Someone put two or more things together which had never been put together before, and likely came across those things as they were wandering aimlessly.

Wander more, and you can take advantage of this as well.

Exercise XIII: Make A Mess

Let's make a mess to innovate.

Recently, I read an article in the latest Wired magazine about tidying up – there is a Japanese author named Marie Kondo who wrote the bestselling "The Life-Changing Magic of Tidying Up" which, I hear, is still on bestselling books lists everywhere, it also seems to be in every airport bookstore I've been in lately. It and her other books discuss how your life will change if you would only tidy up. I'm assuming that with this, and shows like Hoarders, we are seeing a backlash against clutter. She is really against clutter, in fact, discusses in which order you should get rid of stuff (books first, then clothes, then papers, then sentimental objects) and you should only hold onto whatever "brings you joy." Her method is to take everything in the house of that one type, say books, then pile them up in one place, then physically pick up each book and hold it in your hand. If it brings you joy in some way, when you see the book or hold the book, you should keep it, if not, get rid of it.

Now, as someone who, in probably anyone's parlance, hoards books, this is tough advice. Simply looking over at my bookshelf while I'm the middle of thinking through a problem, inventing new things, or simply letting my mind wander, might let me cast my glance across a book title, think about that book, maybe grab it, flip through it again, and glean some new (or refresh some old) insight, which would help me solve the problem, trigger a new invention (maybe by throwing it into the idea blender) or who knows what else. My books are thought triggers, conceptual post-it's in a way, which can be combined with new problems to come up with new solutions. When my books surround me, I feel that I can be more creative.

There are studies to corroborate this: it's no wonder why artists, writers, and creatives seem to flourish in cluttered or messy spaces, it turns out that it if you want to be more creative, you go into a messy space. Cluttered spaces are good for creativity because they help you to trigger new thinking and new combinations, but they sap energy. The opposite is also true – neat spaces are great for productivity, they might not help you come up with creative solutions, but they will help your team to work faster and longer and more diligently. If you want your team to come up with creative solutions or innovative new products, put them in a cluttered, messy space.

Ideally, you want to have both types of spaces in your offices:

- A messy, cluttered space with toys and things to play with together (why not have fun and stock with books (science fiction, fiction and non-fiction), toys, LEGO blocks (not the sets, just the blocks) drawing materials, and stuff, like the Stanford design thinking materials where you can get your hands dirty and just build stuff) where you and your team goes in order to do some creative problem solving,

- an orderly, neat space, where you take the ideas that you generated in the creative space and get them built. You need both the messy space and the orderly space, the best of both worlds, to get the benefit of both.

Exercise XIV: Change the Nouns

Innovate by triggering simple semantic shifts.

There is no need for completely new thinking to create disruptive and innovative products. Completely new thinking can sometimes be difficult, requiring a completely different growth mindset, environment, and team. It's something you may not have access to or be able to whip up at a moment's notice when you need some innovation to occur, or a challenge to solve.

In these cases, there are some simple ways in which you can innovate, help unlock new thinking, just by doing some semantic shifting, a subset of which we call "changing the nouns."

For example, when the web first started, it was a reasonable size, but it was difficult to find what you wanted. Enter the directory – places like Yahoo! and DMOZ, a type of a home page of the internet, where you could find hand curated websites by traversing or searching a directory. It was a directory, with a search, but just for the engine. Later, via Alta Vista, Google, and other engines, these search engines became the "portal" to the internet. Once the portals got to a certain size, then they got to be a little unwieldy, the system of capturing things that were of interest to you is limited to local bookmarks which you stored on your computer.

Eventually, Yahoo! and others invented the concept of the internet, customized to you. Sites like "My Yahoo!" allowed you to see a customized directory, based on your preferred settings. It was "the internet customized to you."

So how do you innovate to get a something like Facebook? You swap the nouns "internet" and "you" and get "you, customized to the internet." Facebook was all about you – your profile and presenting your profile to the world, allowng you to connect with others. Even the name harkens back to the original concept of a "face book, " a paper book full of people's profiles (typically students), helping you to connect with them. Where directories and search engines were all about bringing the internet to you, Facebook is about bringing you to the internet.

There are hundreds of startups and apps out there which are the "uber of X," where X is your favorite noun. I came across a site the other day of a company which only develops "clones" of pre-existing services, I'm assuming hoping to capture some of the marketplaces. But I digress.

Just take a typical phrase, and swap out the nouns, and see what happens. Sometimes you will get nonsense, sometimes you will get nothing new, and other times you will get something completely new that you have never thought of before. Use tools like the Random Word Generator and create new, unexpected combinations. You will innovate.

For example, let's try the random noun generator for "Uber for X."

- member

- extent

- woman

- mom

- attention

How about a "uber for moms," delivering a mom to you when you need a mom type task completed? Or a "uber for attention," delivering someone's attention when you need it? Let's try again:

- estate

- soup

- teacher

- desk

- development

Soup delivery? Teacher delivery? Desk Delivery? Development Delivery? Some of those could fly.

The idea here is not to generate the idea – it's to generate uncommon semantic juxtapositions, which can then trigger new thinking.

Blogging, podcasting, and YouTube were born when someone swapped the "professionals" and "public" when talking about writing, radio, and TV. Swapping "the crowd" for any market which is currently locked down by professionals is one idea.

Try it yourself – take something that you do, or would like to do, and swap out the nouns for new ones, or swap them around completely. You never know what you will create.

Exercise XV: Think Like A Kid

To innovate: be a kid again

When it comes to new, innovative, out-of-the-box thinking, you can't beat kids. I mean, not all kids, but those fearless try-anything-because-they-don't-know not-to kinds of kids. I think you know the kinds of kids I'm thinking of:

1. The ones that climbed up to the roof with their blankets to see if they use them as capes to fly

2. The ones that would take electronic things apart and put them back together

3. The ones that always asked: "why?"

While most of the kids who think out of the box don't understand where the box is – like having beginners mind – there is one key difference between having beginners mind and "kid mind" – it is the unabashed playfulness. The willingness to try something out, just for fun, to see what happens. It's active, assertive, open-mindedness. And of all the tools in our arsenal of innovation, this one is probably the easiest to uncover.

Once we are grownups, we decide that we need to be "professionals." As professionals, we need to act a certain, adult way. We need to use big words and acronyms and do things like "have meetings" and "operationalize strategy" and "organize deliverables" and "gain alignment."

In the Star Trek Original Series episode, Mirror, Mirror, a team from the Enterprise gets transported through a portal to a barbaric "mirror universe" where the good guys are the bad guys and vice versa. While our intrepid team of good guys can easily act more barbaric to fit into the mirror universe, our Spock can very swiftly see that he's got the wrong Kirk, McCoy, Scotty, and Uhura on board, and immediately throws them into the brig. When our good guys are back on our side of the portal, Kirk asks how Spock was able to tell the difference. He points out that the civilized man can always act like a barbarian since he used to be one, where the barbarian has no experience acting like a civilized man.

We all have a child within us. We all used to be one. We can all tap that inner child.

This exercise does just that. Simply cast your mind back to when you were a kid. Become a kid. Act like a kid. Imagine yourself as a kid – with that active, assertive open-mind – that fearless sense that you can do anything.

Imagine that anything is possible. That you can start from nothing, there are no barriers; there is nothing that you think you cannot do. Nothing is stopping you. What ideas come into your head? What would you do – what could you do – if there was nothing to stop you – and you had no fear.

- There is no need to show profits since you aren't even thinking about money.

- There is no need to think about the rules because you don't understand that there are any.

- There is no need to think about the "how" of something, just the "why" of it

Try this at home – and see what your inner child can dream up.

Exercise XVI: Repurposing

Repurposing: it's not just for trash, anymore.

One of the most effective exercises that we use in our innovation sessions is to take an object – any object with a current purpose – and ideate around other purposes and uses for that object.

For example, Tesla's use of an array of individual laptop style batteries instead of GMs and other use of monolithic purpose build batteries for something like the Chevy Volt, clearly show the differences between disruptive and incremental innovation. While the use of a battery array allows Tesla a way to repurpose a common battery form factor, it can also allow for more variations in design, although Tesla has not strayed too far from the very common automotive form factors of sedan and SUV. GM would need to develop a completely different battery form factor for upcoming cars. Additionally, Tesla's design allows the use of those same batteries in home-based arrays, storing solar power.

The basis of many patent applications at the core is the ability to take a concept or object from one sphere and transpose it into another.

It is more than just Uber for X, but to move something which is common in field A, apply it to Field B, and then see what shakes out. I liken it to an author creating characters, placing them in situations, and then allowing the characters to deal with the situation at hand. For example,

I liken it to an author creating characters, placing them in situations, and then allowing the characters to deal with the situation at hand.

For example, let's take common whiteboard markers and place them into a context of food. Maybe develop flavored (not just scented) markers which can draw flavors onto food? If the markers contained sufficiently high-end materials, I see no reason chefs would not be able to use them in haute cuisine.

Or apply the Uber model to garage band musicians – maybe those bands would love to start to build an audience of followers by inviting them to their garages to listen in on practice and jam sessions. There is no limit to the interesting juxtapositions and combinations which you may be able to generate during this exercise. However, I can already sense many of you suggesting that this would not be a useful exercise, generating unprofitable ideas and wasting the ideators time. Taking objects which are common in one field and brainstorming their use in other fields is an effective way to generate new thinking. They may not directly lead to new product ideas, but they do succeed in opening your people's minds to new ideas.

Postscript

While Tesla may have innovated in its use of batteries, it has not innovated in the types of vehicles that it has created, simply creating typical vehicles which fit directly into the expected molds. Personally, this tells me that Tesla is in a similar position to Apple – they may have innovated to get their flagship products off the ground, but after their initial disruption, they maintained a core steady-state of incremental innovation. As innovators, we all know that there is no such thing as a steady-state, and both Tesla and Apple will need to generate some disruption in the short term (as is rumored with Apple) to maintain or regain their position on innovation.

Exercise XVII: Ask "Why Do We Still…"

With all the new technologies and ways of doing things seemingly better and faster, do you ever wonder why we sometimes cling to the old ways of doing things? Why, if much better options are available, do we still do things a certain way? Why do we hesitate to innovate?

We get hired to moderate and facilitate a lot of workshops, meetings, and events. Sometimes, they are focused innovation workshops, centered on developing products and services which can be developed and launched today. Sometimes they have targeted IP generation sessions, expressly designed to generate protectable IP, in the form of patent applications (and hopefully patents). Sometimes, they are far future strategy sessions which can generate all the above. In all our sessions, we also generate massive improvements in employee engagement.

We tend to use repeatable, useful, and mind-expanding session formats, to generate the biggest return in the shortest period. One of the most useful tools in our arsenal is the "Why do we still…" format, which we find fun, engaging and helps to open the team's minds to new possibilities.

In this game, we spend a few minutes generating the end of the question "Why do we still…" – Typically first using individual ideation, then group ideation, then dot voting to select the top three sentence ends. We then randomly split the team into two, and have each team argue for and against this assertion, looking at cultural, social, technical, and other markers to answer the question. We also ask the team to develop a sales pitch for their viewpoint and have the teams compete against each other to determine a winner.

Here are some examples:

- Why do we still buy DVD players? (electronics manufacturer)
- Why do we still use websites? (bank)
- Why do we still use remote controls? (virtual audio assistant

developer)

A good example question for a book retailer might be "Why do we still read paper books?"

The pro side could argue that the physical manifestation of a book is still important to the customer, that tactile sense of the book itself, the feel, the smell, the ease of viewing, all contribute to an all-around pleasurable experience. That side could also argue that the quality of eBooks is sub-par, screens are difficult for some to read, and that for some eBooks, especially those with charts and graphs, they translate to electronic form very poorly. Additionally, they can discuss how to encourage those who prefer eBooks to try instead to use paper books, by highlighting those elements, targeting that market. Finally, they develop a paper book pitch, to be delivered to eBook customers, convincing them to try paper books.

The other side could argue that the electronic delivery of books can be much more rapid, the price of the books is much cheaper as there are no physical elements to the book. They could argue that eBook reader devices are getting better and can present the book in a much more flexible way than just as an analog book. They can argue that paper books are heavier and use up natural resources in production (even if they use recycled paper) so that it is much more environmentally friendly. In the same way as above, the pro-eBook team builds a pitch for eBooks.

When the pitches are complete, they present to each other, and the sides then pick a winner. The exercise is to focus on why, when technology and culture can move us in one direction, they tend to keep us moving in the same direction. It's a great exercise for companies in distress, looking to decide of a pivot or a way in which to redefine their current offerings.

Who knows – you may even be able to discover your next unicorn.

Exercise XVIII: Think Further Out

Expand your time horizon – think further out.

When we ran our first enterprise-wide innovation program, we were gathering all sorts of great ideas from our client employees, but something was missing. After launching the program and running it for a while, it became obvious that most of the ideas generated were incremental features which were simply new add-ons to existing products – extensions which would make products better, improve the customer experience, make a little more money and refinements. There was a category for out-of-the-box ideas, and mashups (where they would blend two or more ideas – see the idea blender) but we didn't get a lot of hugely disruptive breakthrough ideas. They didn't think further out.

We needed a new plan – some way to get people thinking about truly new, disruptive and game-changing ideas.

Right around that time, the company was celebrating their 10th birthday. Part of that was a yearlong celebration of all things about the company; they had told stories about the company's history. They printed up a large commemorative photo book detailing the history of the company, from the early days when the founders would have to sleep under their desks in their cubes at their first office in Mountain View, to getting into the Guinness Book of World Records, all the way to the present day, where 12,000+ employees where creating cool new products. The photo book ended with a montage of everyone who currently worked there, and then at the very end, a blank page. A blank page, for all the employees to complete. A space to map out the next ten years.

When I saw that blank page, I had a thought myself: while it's great to look back ten years over the course of history, what if we took ALL employees and asked them to look ten years forward instead? What if we ran an internal, crowdsourced, foresight program asking people to put their minds into the year 2017. To try to envision not only what the company would be like in 10 years, but what the internet would be like, what interfaces would be like, what the industry would be like, what their customers would be like, and finally, what would the world be like? After pitching this to the CEO directly, we got the go ahead, and built out a program which we literally "set" 10 years out – we developed what we called a "Futurist" program. With the assistance of the Institute for The Future, we came up with "artifacts from the future," styled all the materials in a cool, fun retro-future way, and during the month-long program, posted blog posts from the year 2017. We were able to help them think further out.

The program was a huge success, generating a ton of excitement and ideas, and we had a lot of fun running it. In the end, a lot of the ideas were perfectly suited for induction into the patent program we were running, so not only did we fire up the organization to think with more of an eye to the future, we built out a lot of interesting new product ideas, many very disruptive. Some of the ideas we patented in 2007 ended up in products like Magic Leap's AR goggles.

Since then, we've run this exercise several times, and I can tell you that we always have great results. Even though you ask people to think ten years out, most of the time the ideas end up in that sweet spot between fantasy and what you can build today, probably about five years out, which is great for setting your future strategy.

ABOUT THE AUTHOR

Chris Kalaboukis is a disruptive visionary innovator, prolific inventor, speaker, and futurist. He is the co-founder of helloFUTURE, a global foresight, innovation, and patent development consultancy specializing in the development of innovative new products, services, patents and strategies for financial services, technology, media, and retail/e-commerce companies. He is also named on over 70 patents in the internet, social networking, and fintech space. An experienced technologist and coder, he has architected, developed, and launched a multitude of apps, both web, and mobile. A serial entrepreneur, he has helmed several startups from inception to launch. He has authored several books on innovation and the future and blogs and podcasts at thinkfuture.com

LET'S TALK

Thanks for reading.

What is your greatest innovation challenge?

Let's figure it out together.

Contact me here:

- chris@hellofuture.co
- http://linkedin.com/in/thinkfuture
- http://hellofuture.co

Thanks...Chris

www.ingramcontent.com/pod-product-compliance
Lightning Source LLC
Chambersburg PA
CBHW071028240526
45469CB00006BD/2139